The Identity
of Suffolk

The essence of Suffolk: an isolated farmstead at Worlingworth Green.

The Identity of Suffolk

Celia Jennings

SUFFOLK PRESERVATION SOCIETY

© Suffolk Preservation Society 1980

First published 1980 by Suffolk Preservation Society
Little Hall, Market Place,
Lavenham, Sudbury,
Suffolk CO10 9QZ

ISBN 0 9502293 6 9

Photoset in Palatino by
Rowland Phototypesetting Limited
Bury St Edmunds, Suffolk
and printed in Great Britain by
St Edmundsbury Press, Bury St Edmunds, Suffolk

This book was commissioned by the Suffolk Preservation
Society to mark its fiftieth anniversary. The views
expressed in it are not necessarily those of the Executive
Committee of the Society.

Contents

Foreword

When the Suffolk Preservation Society was formed fifty years ago, Suffolk was still a fundamentally rural county. Its enormous wealth of medieval churches, handsome timber-framed buildings, hedgerows and trees, the legacy of a once prosperous and highly cultivated past, was still fairly untouched by the outside world. But it was also particularly vulnerable to change. A county without building stone which relies so heavily on easily destroyed timber for its buildings and hedges for its field boundaries can quickly be made unrecognizable; and its situation close to the heavily populated south-east of England has made it a target for resettlement in the last three decades.

This book describes the changes that have taken place since the foundation of the Suffolk Preservation Society from a particular viewpoint. It has not necessarily been written with the idea of pleasing the professional planner or of satisfying the expert conservationist. It is rather a personal account for those for whom planning and legislation are only valuable if they achieve their objectives. The beautifully produced plans, the carefully researched appraisals, the pains-taking traffic surveys are meaningless if they do not create acceptable results for those who have to live with them. Therefore this is, on the whole, the story of what *has* happened in Suffolk, rather than of what the authorities intended should happen, and it is written for people who respond to feeling rather than theory.

My commission from the Executive Committee of the Suffolk Preservation Society was to write its history. The choice of examples was left entirely to me, and I have taken those which seemed to be characteristic of the way in which the Society was working at each phase of its history. I am very conscious that I have needed to be highly selective in mentioning the many people who have played an important role in the life of the Society; the danger of including too large and confusing a cast for the general reader to assimilate has always been before me. However, I feel bound to pay tribute here to the late Leslie Dow, whose erudition contributed so much to the Executive Committee; and to the late Norman Smedley, also a committee member for many years and later the first Director of the Museum of East Anglian Life at Stowmarket. For the same reason, there has been no space to mention in the text a number of people who have contributed much to the County and District Planning Departments. Their work is documented, sometimes anonymously, in the list of plans and surveys which forms Appendix Eight.

I am most grateful to the Executive Committee of the Society and also to many other members for their support and help during the writing of this book; and in particular to Mr E. Field Reid, who first suggested the book to me and whose constant assistance has been invaluable. Also I would like to thank Mr Hugh Paget, Chairman of the SPS at the inception of the book, Miss Dorothy Goslett, the Hon. Secretary, and Mr George Coulson, the Membership Secretary, for much advice and comment. Without the help of the Director of the Society, Mr John Popham, I should have been quite unable to tackle much of the recent history and most of the appendices.

I am deeply indebted to many people who have spared the time to discuss the SPS and conservation generally, among them the Earl of Stradbroke, Patron of the SPS, the Duke of Grafton, President of the SPS, Mr Desmond Pakenham, present Chairman of the SPS, Sir Joshua Rowley, Mr Anthony Foord, Mr Henry Engleheart, Lady Kirwan, Mrs C. G. Brocklebank, Mrs John Agate and Mr Norman Collinson; also to the many members of the SPS district committees who supplied me with detailed information about the county. I owe a special debt of gratitude to Mr David Dymond and to Mr Norman Scarfe who provided helpful and constructive comment on the text.

I am greatly indebted to the ready assistance of members of the Planning Department of Suffolk County Council, particularly Mr Cyril Garnham, Mr Christopher Stratton and Miss Melinda Appleby. Also to the staff of the Planning Department of Ipswich Borough Council and the District Councils of Babergh, Forest Heath, Mid-Suffolk, St Edmundsbury, Suffolk Coastal and Waveney for patiently answering questions and providing me with appendix material.

For assistance with the early history of the Society, I must thank Mr Seymour Schofield, who also provided some photographs, Mrs Sydney Schofield, Mrs Monica Dance, lately secretary of the SPAB, Mr T. B. Oxenbury, Mr F. Bridgeman, Mrs Joyce Bluss of the CPRE, Mrs K. Monnington, and in particular the Rev. Canon W. M. Lummis, whose lively memory at the age of ninety-three was of the greatest assistance.

I am deeply grateful to Mrs Edwin Smith for her generosity in allowing me to use photographs by her late husband; and also to Mr John Mead, Mr Kenneth Gilbert, Dr Alan Beaumont and Dr John Agate for photographs.

I have had the ready co-operation of Christina Newns who did the drawings, and of Elizabeth Cazalet who drew the maps.

I must acknowledge my debt to many experts in various fields, including Mr Anthony Barker, Mr Howard Newby and Mr David Rose of the University of Essex for giving me the benefit of their thoughts on conservation; Miss Anne Page, for the history of the Suffolk Naturalists Society; Group Captain F. W. Sledmere of the Suffolk Trust for Nature Conservation; the Nature Conservancy Council and Mr Edgar Milne-Redhead for information on nature reserves; Squadron Leader J. N. Bloomfield for checking the airfield map; many other people for answering a number of small queries; and the Suffolk Record Office staff for their help.

I am very grateful for Sir John Betjeman's permission to reprint his *Daily Telegraph* article, 'Urbs in Rure' (Appendix Thirteen); to the *East Anglian Magazine* for Mrs Schofield's and John Suffolk's articles (Appendix Twelve); to Mr Robert Maltster and the *East Anglian Daily Times* for photographs and press cuttings; and to *Punch* for the cartoons on pages 31, 43 and 49.

East Bergholt, July 1980.

List of Illustrations

Maps

Lavenham in a simpler age, with roads unsurfaced and lit by gas lamps. The Swan Inn plaster-covered on the right at the bottom of the hill and unrecognizable before its extensive re-modelling.

1 The Suffolk Scene: The Background

The boundaries of Suffolk, mostly rivers, tell us that *over there* is foreign territory: Norfolk, the county that has given all schoolchildren the mistaken idea that the whole of East Anglia is flat; Essex and Cambridgeshire, both with hidden delights so unjustly unexplored because of our hurry to get to London or Cambridge. In the centre of these sits Suffolk, its ancient division into east and west now officially removed but still lingering firmly in the imagination of its older inhabitants.

Suffolk is a county which can be fully appreciated only after long familiarity. The casual visitor, though he may be faintly aware that the horizon is widening as he approaches the border from Colchester, may easily say, as Constable's small daughter did on crossing the Stour at Stratford St Mary into her father's beloved childhood country, 'Oh, it is only fields.' It may take a lifetime to gain a real understanding of this essentially gentle landscape which stretches, with subtle variations, from the low shingle beaches of the eastern shore through the heavy clay and deep ditches of central Suffolk to the strange sandy Breckland and the chalky heaths of Newmarket.

Suffolk, like all other English counties, has been shaped by its history, and many of the features that mystify a stranger can be explained (and are becoming more and more understood as the disciples of Professor W. G. Hoskins increase) by the social and agricultural customs of the past. The villages are perhaps most puzzling to those used to the 'typical English village' with its manor house, church and pub neatly arranged round the village green.

Even with the aid of archaeology, place-name studies, maps and the overall history of the county, it may be difficult to understand the complexity of the villages, the subtle differences of the regions, and their varying phases of development over the centuries. Those parishes (most common on the heavy land of central Suffolk) where single farmsteads are dotted about the landscape, with an isolated church and perhaps a small group of buildings close to it, seem at first sight to belong to a different order from the more familiar thoroughfare villages like Stratford St Mary or Long Melford, where the houses line the street on either side of an important road. The newcomer may well be confused by places like Cockfield, with its numerous small greens with houses round them, and find it hard to believe that they are all part of the same parish. Mellis, for instance, or Barking, with their immense commons, are more intelligible; and many of the West Suffolk villages seem by comparison straightforward enough in appearance.

But it is disconcerting to find, once one's mind is made up about the layout of some particular place, that it does not fall so simply into a single category; that one may turn a corner and find the pattern has changed over the centuries and is indeed still changing; that a nineteenth-century estate has created a new village close to the old, with cottages for its employees built in a style quite alien to the older buildings, though, to our modern eyes, now almost equally admirable.

Kersey. The small medieval manufacturing town opens straight on to fields. A rare survival almost untouched by modern development.

What do we think of first when we hear the word 'Suffolk'? Some may, with a memory of childhood holidays by the sea, think of Aldeburgh or Southwold, those sandy-tracked heathlands covered with gorse and heather, the shingle beaches and the grey-blue sea and sparkling light that Wilson Steer caught so perfectly in his paintings at the turn of the century. The Waveney valley, with its feathery willows and its houses with their purplish-black pantiled roofs, may be the image that comes into the minds of others. The gentle slopes of the Stour valley, the open views of the Breckland, ancient woodlands seen across cornfields – all of these crowd out of the mind the twentieth-century blight of Haverhill or Great Cornard. But the first thing that comes across our vision is the farmstead, alone in the middle of the fields, its steep roof, tiled or thatched, glimpsed through its protective trees – the essence of the Suffolk man's desire for privacy.

Suffolk's customary systems of inheritance and division of property between heirs must account for at least some of the many scattered farmhouses in the landscape. The number of small manors, often several in one parish, perhaps explains the absence of great houses (only Heveningham and Ickworth on the really grand scale) and the presence of innumerable smaller but substantial houses of the farmer or merchant turned country gentleman of the late Middle Ages.

In the fifteenth and the first half of the sixteenth century, the manufacture of cloth was of great economic importance in Suffolk. At that time large amounts of cloth were made and exported, the wealth created by the trade being reflected in the houses and churches surviving from that period. The trade began to decline in the seventeenth century and was finally overtaken by the growing textile industries in the Midlands and North of England.

Commerce created the middle classes. How important they are to the development of Suffolk's landscape – indeed, to the landscape of the whole of England, for it was they who brought about those rapid changes in industry, transport and local government which mark the beginnings of the story of the struggle to keep Suffolk's undervalued beauty alive, and it was they who were later in the forefront of the movement to preserve that beauty when it was threatened with destruction.

In 1888 Suffolk's division into East Suffolk and West Suffolk was formally recognized by the creation of the respective county councils under the Local Government Act. The dividing line between the two halves of the county had existed as an administrative boundary for at least eight centuries, the great liberty of St Edmund on the west being separated from the eastern half by the line following the old hundred boundaries. The division was one of economic convenience fought for in the House of Lords on behalf of the people of West Suffolk by the Marquess of Bristol, the owner of the Ickworth estate, in order to protect them from the higher rates that might be forced on the whole county by their more prosperous neighbours in the east.

Apart from farming, what industry there was in Suffolk in the eighteenth and nineteenth centuries had been concentrated mainly on the eastern side, where transport up the main highways was reasonably good and the rail service excellent. Outside Ipswich, the smaller towns of Leiston, Halesworth, Beccles and Lowestoft were, by Suffolk standards, well provided with regular work in the breweries and the corn trade which offered the traditional commercial outlets. Employment was also provided by the manufacturers of agricultural machinery

Medieval timber-framed farmhouse and thatched barn at Hacheston; one of hundreds on the heavy clay land of central Suffolk.

whose firms grew up in the early nineteenth century. Ransomes of Ipswich, Garretts of Leiston and Smyths of Peasenhall had become world famous, and, in Beccles and Bungay, were well-known printing works.

By contrast, West Suffolk, though it had some manufacturing industry in Bury St Edmunds, Haverhill and other smaller places, was more dependent on agriculture for employment, and its workers often had only seasonal work on the farms. The successive agricultural depressions, though they affected all farm labourers, brought about a greater concentration of hardship in the west.

These agricultural depressions, which were common in the nineteenth century, continued into the first quarter of the twentieth, apart from a boom during the First World War, until a change, both in crops and the mechanization of farming, brought some relief. Agricultural changes were nothing new to Suffolk. In the late medieval period, dairying developed strongly, and the need for hedging land to keep in the stock had subdivided even further the already fragmented fields. By the eighteenth century, corn was the main crop, though there was still a good deal of pasture for the hornless Suffolk cattle to graze. But arable farming became an uncertain source of livelihood. The Napoleonic Wars encouraged high grain prices and even more land was turned over to arable; the fortunes of grain fluctuated wildly throughout the rest of the country. The repeal of the Corn Laws of the 1840s allowed cheap foreign corn to be imported, and although the Crimean War encouraged home production, the bad harvests of the 1870s once more brought disaster to many farmers. By the end of the century, Suffolk had become one of the poorest and most depressed counties in England.

It was not until 1925, when the comparatively new crop, sugar beet, was given official recognition with the Beet Sugar Subsidy Act, that farming began to take an upward turn again. Where there had once been herds of grazing cows and sheep, or fields of wheat or barley, there were now acres of beet – still grown, on the whole, in the small fields enclosed in medieval and Tudor times, their hedgerows still intact.

The changes that were taking place in Suffolk in the 1920s must have been baffling to those who could think back to the previous century. An old man would have been able to remember Ipswich at a time when it was almost as Dickens knew it, when it was full of gardens with green gates, like the one through which Job Trotter advanced on Sam Weller. Those who were still young could remember a time before motor transport when the road surfaces in the country were little better than they had been hundreds of years before. A county surveyor described them as being repaired

> . . . by broken stone, in many cases picked from fields and broken on the side of the road by hand; the stone was applied direct to the road surface and ground in by traffic. Men were continually employed with rakes in pulling the stones into the ruts or tracks which naturally formed. . . . Sand was scraped from the road and placed on the top of the loose stone to help to bind it in and hold it together. In some cases faggots would be placed in the ruts and they would then be covered with gravel and flints.

This surface, as well as being uncomfortable to drive on, threw up dust in summer

Marshland below Orford: Havergate Island.

and mud in winter. Those beautiful roadside hedgerows that we now set so much store by, where they still survive, may sometimes have been covered with white dust and grime and probably seldom looked anything like the picturesque boundaries of our imagination.

In 1920 many of these roads still followed, without alteration, the pattern that they had followed for hundreds of years. Those tortuous twisting lanes once marked the edges of countless small estates and farms, bounded by deep ditches

Badley Church and Hall: remote and peaceful, though busy Stowmarket is only three miles away.

which served for drainage as well as for boundaries. The need for by-passes had not yet come, though the county councils were beginning to turn their attention to the reconstruction of the main roads, and, as these improved, the flow of commercial and holiday traffic increased. Greater mobility brought more of the middle class from the towns to the country; until that time far fewer people lived in the remote country or the smaller villages from choice, however delightful those villages may have seemed. But with a car and easy access to Ipswich or Bury St Edmunds, for shopping or dinner parties, many of those who had lived in the well-to-do parts of these towns made their homes in the surrounding villages.

East Suffolk seems always to have had the advantage of easy transport, partly because of its two main roads thrusting northwards, and its railway system which, by the first quarter of the twentieth century, allowed for a quicker journey to London (about an hour and a half from Ipswich, as opposed to Bury St Edmunds's two and a half). Even within the counties, it was quicker to go from Haverhill to Ipswich by train than from Haverhill to Bury St Edmunds – half the distance as the crow flies. But with so many of the villages and small towns provided with stations, there was plenty of opportunity for country people to work in town and, in the first quarter of the twentieth century, there was a sharp decline in the number of village shops which, coupled with the use of the internal combustion

Coastal erosion at Covehithe Cliffs.

engine on the roads and the introduction of mechanized farming methods, caused radical changes in the way country people lived.

With so many alterations in town and country in the early part of this century, it was probably difficult for most people to grasp the effect of this change on the familiar scenes. So much happened, and it happened so quickly. Attached as many were to their old towns and villages and to the countryside round about, there seemed to be little they could do as factories began to encroach on rural areas, new houses went up and trees disappeared. And had they wished to protest, there was no one to protest *to*. The only buildings that had any statutory protection at all were a small number of ancient monuments. There were no planning laws. A man could, provided he owned the site, put up any building he liked, regardless of size or suitability. Any great house in England could have been pulled down. Such houses as Blenheim, Hatfield or Ickworth could have disappeared, and, of course, some great houses did; in Suffolk, Rushbrooke Hall was demolished as late as 1961. Any preservation or protection that there was had to be done by voluntary societies.

Anthony Barker's comprehensive survey, *The Local Amenity Movement*, undertaken for the Civic Trust, shows how few these societies were before the late 1950s. Apart from the Sidmouth Improvement Committee, founded in 1846 before any national organization, only a handful appeared in the nineteenth century, and the Dartmoor Preservation Society, founded in 1883, seems to have been the only one covering a large area. In the main, before the foundation of the Society for the Protection of Ancient Buildings (SPAB), in 1877, and the National Trust in 1895, it had been individuals who protested about acts of vandalism, though it is hard to find examples before the seventeenth century.

The earliest people to stir up public indignation seem, not surprisingly, all to have been writers. John Aubrey had a practical method of saving Broadchalke church: he had himself made a churchwarden. Dr Johnson quoted a fellow writer in his complaint against the eighteenth-century city fathers of Lichfield:

> Evelyn, in his book of forest trees, tells of wicked men that cut down trees and never prospered afterwards, yet nothing has deterred these audacious Aldermen from violating the Hamadryads of George Lane.

This is a grievance only too familiar to modern conservationists.

Suffolk, too, has had its early protectors. There was John Constable, protesting about the felling of an ancient elm in East Bergholt; and there was Nathaniel Bloomfield, lamenting the loss of the tiny green at Honington by Parliamentary Enclosure in a long, clumsy, but moving poem:

> The Green was our pride through the year
>   For in spring, when the wild flow'rets blew,
> Tho' many rich pastures were near,
>   Where cowslips and daffodils grew;
> And tho' such gallant flow'rs were our choice,
>   It was interrupted by fear —

Suffolk's shifting coastline. Orford was a flourishing port until the silting up of the river in the sixteenth century.

The fear of their Owner's dread voice,
    Harshly bawling, 'You've no business here!'

While the Green, tho' but daisies its boast
    Was free as the flow'rs to the bee
In all seasons the Green we lov'd most,
    Because on the Green we were free.
'Twas the prospect that first met my eyes,
    And memory still blesses the scene,
For early my heart learnt to prize
    The freedom on Honington Green.

And so on for fifteen more verses, surely the longest celebration of one acre of land in the whole of English literature.

One of the few benefits to the public that the nineteenth century brought to Ipswich was initiated by the sale of Christchurch Mansion and Park in 1894 and the proposal to demolish the mansion and develop the area for housing. Felix Cobbold, then MP for the Stowmarket division of Suffolk and a member of the well-known family of brewers, persuaded the Corporation to buy the estate as a public park and museum.

Breckland. The landscape transformed in the twentieth century with chalk workings and Forestry Commission plantations.

No doubt there were many people, without the financial means or the gift of expression, who shared the feelings of these protesters, but, in Suffolk at least, it was not until 1912 that there was any kind of joint resistance to the destruction of the familiar environment. About that time, some of Suffolk's finer buildings were being sold and transported to other parts of the country. A magnificent sixteenth-century building from Carr Street, Ipswich, was removed, first to the White City Exhibition of 1908 in London, and later to Northamptonshire. Some houses were even bought and shipped home by romantically inclined Americans. A county full of timber-framed buildings was an easy target for such enterprises. Removal is a comparatively easy task with timber-framed buildings; the frames were made in a carpenter's yard, parts numbered and put together on the site. It is necessary only to remove the infilling of wattle and daub and the coatings of lime-plaster, take the frame to pieces and re-erect it on the new site.

This fate had already befallen several houses in Suffolk, but when, in 1912, the

inhabitants of Lavenham saw the fifteenth-century Wool Hall being dismantled, they called a public meeting at the school to protest against its removal. An enterprising local man, seeing that their efforts had been unavailing, resolved to follow the vehicle which was taking the frame to its new destination. Having found out where the building had gone, he approached Princess Louise, Duchess of Argyll, known for her sympathy towards preservation, who bought the building back from the purchaser and had it restored to its original position. But Lavenham has always been a special case, the focal point of attention in Suffolk, its Guildhall cited in the histories of the development of building long before the town became the showplace that it is today.

It is interesting to note that in the same year as the Lavenham incident, 1912, Basil Oliver published his pioneering book, *Old Houses and Village Buildings in East Anglia*, which laid the foundations for the serious study of timber-framed buildings in the region.

Apart from the Lavenham example, it is hard to find any evidence of a concerted effort to conserve either buildings or landscape in Suffolk in the early twentieth century, though Norfolk, with the formation of the Norwich Society in 1923, was ahead of the times. England as a whole had no champion for its landscape, apart from the National Trust, which bought and preserved what it could. It was not until the formation in 1926 of the Council for the Preservation of Rural England (CPRE; the unfashionable word 'Preservation' was changed to 'Protection' in 1969) that the countryside in general became a matter of national concern. It was still only by the efforts of the individual that houses and trees were saved from ruin or

Heveningham Hall. Put up for sale by the government in 1980.

Forestry Commission planting: beautiful in itself but creating the same atmosphere from Scotland to Suffolk.

Wangford Glebe. Birch plantation gives some stability to the wind-swept sands.

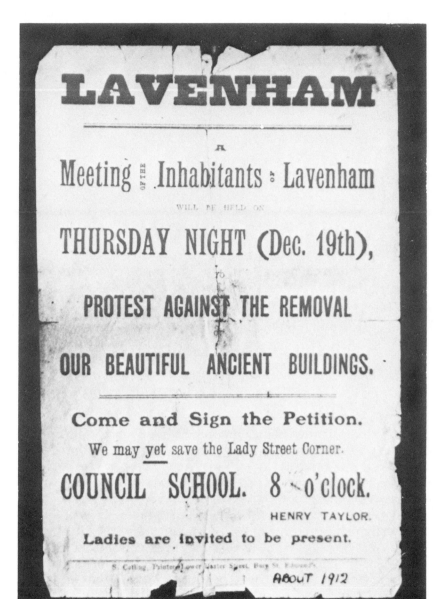

The beginnings of conservation in Lavenham.

Lavenham Wool Hall in the early twentieth century. Built as the hall of the Guild of Our Lady, the central gable was added in the seventeenth century when it was converted to the Wool Hall. It now forms part of the Swan Hotel.

destruction. And, though much of the landscape was still in a state of undisturbed beauty, there was a general air of decay in Suffolk villages. Continual agricultural depressions had left most farmers too poor to keep their houses in good repair. Re-tiling or thatching a roof was an expensive business; a covering of corrugated iron was cheap and weatherproof, though intolerably noisy in wet weather. That it was durable as well as cheap cannot be questioned; some of it has lasted to the present day. Corrugated iron came in useful for fencing in the village pond – still used, since there was no regular refuse collection, for its time-honoured function as a dumping place for all the mattresses, bedsteads and other rubbish which could not be burnt or turned into compost. Sanitation was still of the most primitive kind; as late as 1945 many villages in the county were still without a piped water supply, and not for more than another ten years was main drainage to arrive in the rest of them. There had been improvements, of course, in public health and education and the building of new council houses, but until 1930, when county councils took over the relief of the poor, the workhouses continued to cast their shadow over the unemployed and the destitute.

The land was still, in all places except for the large estates, almost as fragmented as it had been in medieval times. In a village of 2,000 acres there might be as many

The Wool Hall partly demolished in 1912.

as ten or twelve farmers, though here, surely, some used the title as a euphemism for smallholder.

Even the beauty spots were neglected. In 1926 Willy Lott's house, now with Anne Hathaway's cottage probably the best known small house in England, was on the point of collapse. Another victim of agricultural depression, it was saved, just in time, by Mr T. R. Parkington of Ipswich, and extensively restored. It seemed to have been repaired very little since it appeared in Constable's painting 'The Haywain' a hundred years earlier.

The rural population, with all the difficulties of irregular employment and the growing use of machinery in the fields, continued drifting to the towns as it had been doing since the beginning of the century. East Suffolk County Council, in a vain attempt to encourage people to remain in the country, purchased land to be let as smallholdings. But a mere 5,000 acres did little to solve the problem and, between 1921 and 1931, the village population continued to drop while the towns enlarged. The farmhouses and cottages that had often been divided to accommodate the rapidly growing families of the early nineteenth century fell empty all over the county, and buildings that had once been the pride of the prosperous clothier or yeoman farmer became picturesque but desolate ruins.

Willy Lott's House, Flatford, in 1920 . . .

. . . and after its restoration in 1926.

An extravagant combination of art and industry.

The ultimate in corrugated iron at Bawdsey.

2 Early Days

Among the large numbers of dilapidated timber-framed houses was one which was to become the headquarters of a new movement in Suffolk. In 1925, Otley High House attracted the attention of a couple who wished to move to East Anglia from Cornwall. Elmer Schofield was an American, a landscape painter whose early years resemble those of Constable. He was the son of a prosperous mill owner but, being without aptitude for business, had overcome the opposition of his family, studied painting at Julian's in Paris and become well known in America. His wife, Muriel, the daughter of a Lancashire mill owner with an interest in architecture and archaeology, fell in love with the house and persuaded the rather less enthusiastic Mr Schofield to buy it.

Mrs Schofield, then in her mid-fifties, having commissioned her son Sydney to restore High House, began to explore the Suffolk countryside. Unable to drive, she persuaded her gardener or one of her sons to conduct her on trips of inspection, and what she saw convinced her that there was a need for more than the goodwill of a few wealthy people to rescue Suffolk, on the one hand from decay and on the other from the depressing array of electric poles and wires that was beginning to appear. Most of all, she was concerned by the springing up of petrol stations to cope with increasing motor traffic. She began to form the idea of a society which might, she said, influence the 'climate of opinion'.

Her approach was practical. The committee should consist of people who knew about various aspects of Suffolk: architects, archaeologists, businessmen, newspapermen, those who would work and speak with authority. She did not forget the aristocracy, without whom no society in those days was complete, but she made them vice-presidents, along with some of the big landowners and the distinguished clergy. It was a shrewd move which kept everybody happy; the committee being able to get on with the day-to-day business of the society, and the others sufficiently involved to have their interest secured.

The Society got off to a rather slow start. On 9 December 1929, Mrs Schofield, apparently already having decided on the name and arranged its affiliations, wrote on the first page of her minute book:

Suffolk Preservation Society

Affiliated with the Council for the Preservation of Rural England. Associated with the Society for the Protection of Ancient Buildings and The Royal Society of Arts Cottage Fund.

President

The Viscount Ullswater P.C. G.C.B.

Hon. Sec. and Treas.   Chairman
Mrs Elmer Schofield   Major Rowley Elliston MA DL

Muriel Schofield, the founder of the Suffolk Preservation Society, as a young woman.

William Rowley Elliston. Chairman of the Suffolk Preservation Society from its inception until his death in 1953.

Having obtained the assent of twelve proposed vice-presidents, she called a meeting at Otley High House, at which William Rowley Elliston took the chair. It would have been hard to find a more suitable candidate for the office. He had been Mayor of Ipswich the previous year, when he had resigned as Liberal candidate for the Woodbridge division of Suffolk. He wrote leaders for the *East Anglian Daily Times*, and is described in the *Times* by Roger Fulford as 'a man gifted with scholarly charm'. These qualities were combined with a deep love of Suffolk, and he and Mrs Schofield could between them contact a wide range of likely members.

At this stage, no committee was elected, but arrangements were made for the first public meeting to launch the Society at Ipswich Town Hall on 9 January 1930. The speakers were to include A. R. Powys, the Secretary of the Society for the

Protection of Ancient Buildings, and Morley Horder of the Preservation Committee of the Royal Society of Arts.

At this meeting, attended by 'a large audience representative of town and county', Lord Ullswater was elected President and the Committee appointed. Mr Powys made a spirited appeal for the new society to associate itself with other bodies existing to preserve the amenities of the country. His views on the name of the Society may come as something of a surprise to those who imagine the conservationists of the past to have been backward looking. 'It had been proposed to call the new organization the Suffolk Preservation Society, but he considered the name should be such as to give the Society a much wider scope.' Mrs Schofield, however, seems to have been very satisfied with the meeting. 'We ought to have accomplished something with such a launching,' she wrote to Mr Powys the following day.

During the next few months little seems to have been done beyond discussion, but, in July 1930, Bury St Edmunds, 'on the initiative of the Mayor of Bury (Mrs J. W. Greene)', took the unusual step of publicly identifying the town with the SPS. At this gathering, Colonel Carwardine Probert gave an account of the objectives of the Society and, after launching a rather fierce attack on the new Shakespeare Theatre at Stratford-upon-Avon, said: 'Preservation is only a part of our work, and *a desire for decent modern buildings ought to be fostered*': an important point, and one that a few SPS members even now occasionally dispute, though Colonel Probert's idea of decent modern building might now be questioned.

It was nearly a year after the preliminary meeting that the SPS held its first General Meeting at Ipswich Town Hall. The *East Anglian Daily Times* reported that it 'resolved itself into speeches by notabilities upon the sylvan properties of the county, and suggestions whereby things that are beautiful may remain without hindering, or being hindered by, the snowball-like progress of its impedimenta'. The notabilities expressed themselves in a more down-to-earth manner. Mr Pretyman of Orwell Park feared that landowners might, in the near future, be penalized by land value taxation if they retained main road frontages that were unbuilt upon. Lord Ullswater, in a not altogether tactful speech in which he seemed to be comparing Suffolk rather unfavourably with his native county of Westmorland and Cumberland, nevertheless put in a strong plea for the protection of the countryside from ignorance, neglect and indifference. He deplored the unpleasantness of the electricity pylons and cables which were beginning to disfigure the county. The importance of the education of children in 'the glory of their heritage' was stressed by the former headmaster of Winchester, Dr Montague Rendall, and mayors, county council spokesmen, the CPRE and the clergy all joined in supporting the aims of the Society. Mrs Schofield had done her work well. An exhibition of photographs designed to show 'how things should be and should not be' was organized in the Ancient House in Ipswich.

By February 1931, the Society had got into its stride. Meetings were held monthly, normally at the houses of the committee members in turn, the minutes being written out in Mrs Schofield's large, confident and sometimes illegible handwriting. If there is an air of tea and cucumber sandwiches about the recording of these meetings, there was nothing amateurish or over-genteel about the way matters were handled. Mrs Schofield had no hesitation in tackling anyone, from

The Hall of Otley High House (the home of Mrs Schofield) after restoration by Sydney Schofield.

the East Anglian Electric Supply Co. to the most distinguished architects of the day. She secured the support of the Women's Institutes of East and West Suffolk, sent circular letters to all the parish councils in the county asking for their co-operation, campaigned successfully for the removal of ugly advertisements, and was in constant touch with the county councils of East and West Suffolk. Curiously, the Committee seems to have had no dealings with the Suffolk Naturalists Society, also founded in 1929, though its founder, Claude Morley, himself a keen local historian who had initiated its breakaway from the Suffolk Institute of Archaeology and Natural History, was an early member of the SPS and both societies had many members in common. Mrs Schofield's Committee, though it had plenty to say on nature conservation, directed its ideas towards the CPRE.

The Rev. W. M. Lummis, Honorary Secretary of the Suffolk Preservation Society, 1937–47.

Early Cases

Thanks to the helpful publicity given by the local press, the Committee received a flood of letters. Complaints of all kinds flowed in, familiar now to anyone concerned with amenity societies: cottages in danger, 'eyesores', removal of box-pews in Cretingham church, trees at Coddenham 'on the land' belonging to a former vicar who 'seems to take a pleasure in denuding the district of what is its greatest beauty'. But it was the fate of the windmills that caused the greatest agitation. In the mid-1930s, sixty-two Suffolk parishes still had a mill standing, many, of course, in a poor state, but still contributing an important element in the landscape that we have almost completely lost. The Society quickly realized that there was no hope of saving more than a handful; as the next best thing, they put in hand a survey which was carried out by the young Norman Collinson, still a member of the Executive Committee today. He made a report on the condition of each mill and photographed them all; an early and enlightened example of a recording scheme that we nowadays take for granted, but then something of an innovation, though earlier work had been done in this field by the Rev. W. M. Lummis and Arthur Woolnough.

Members of the Conference on Regional and Town Planning at Bonar Law College, Ashridge, Herts in March 1931. Mrs Schofield standing far right.

Newspaper publicity aroused interest in neighbouring counties. At a conference on Regional and Town Planning at Ashridge in March 1931, called by the CPRE, presumably to discuss Hilton Young's proposed Town and Country Planning Act (superseding the 1925 Town Planning Act and the first to refer to country planning), the Suffolk delegates were asked to provide details of the formation of the SPS, as Norfolk and Essex were interested in forming similar societies.

Throughout the early years of the Society, the electrification of the villages took up most of the Committee's time. Everyone wanted electric light, but nobody wanted the hideous wires and poles which so dramatically changed the appearance of the villages. Nothing in history, not even the railways, had made such a rapid impact on the look of things. Lavenham, as always, was the prime cause for concern, though to be fair, the Society fought strenuously whenever possible for the placing underground of electricity cables. Mrs Schofield commented wryly in brackets in her minutes: 'It is unfortunate that there should be in the parish council [of East Bergholt in this case] such apathy before the event and such excitement when the work commences.' No doubt these attitudes were fairly common. It needed some degree of imagination to picture what the result of electrification might be. Mrs Schofield organized a circular letter, 'tastefully got up', to the parish councils, warning them of the damage to the beauty of the countryside, and a little later sent a letter to 'people of note in Suffolk and England generally asking them to sign a petition for underground transmission in Lavenham'. These efforts were not altogether successful; after three years of wrangling with the East Anglian Electricity Company, Lavenham residents were still distressed by the erection of ugly poles in many of their streets, though the Company protested that they had made concessions which had cost them £800. The SPS felt it could do no more.

By the time of the Annual General Meeting, in November 1932, the Society had consolidated its constitution. It announced its objects:

To safeguard the countryside, to protect the aesthetic amenities of towns and villages within the County, and to further the preservation in appropriate settings of buildings whether large or small, which are of historic interest or of picturesque value.

The subscription was to be five shillings a year and the Society was to be managed by an Executive Committee of nine, with power to co-opt. We may assume, though no records exist, that there were about 200 members, judging by the rate of expansion of lists for 1935 and 1937.

The historic interest mentioned in the constitution seems, surprisingly, to have been the least well developed strand in the consciousness of the Society at that time, even though the Executive Committee contained such distinguished local historians as Vincent Redstone, Charles Partridge (founder, in 1901, of the *East Anglian Miscellany*, that gold mine for all local historians) and the Rev. Edmund Farrer, whose scholarly works are still in constant use in the Suffolk Record Office. It might be reasonable to conclude, from some of their dealings, that the members were intent on keeping Suffolk a picturesque and rather romantic country, and had little real interest in its past as a vital industrial and agricultural part of England. Certainly the Committee had no hesitation in applauding Sir Cuthbert Quilter's demolition in Lavenham of 'three small cottages which formerly obscured the Hall and the Gild of Corpus Christi on the Market Place and described in the Court Rolls as "3 small tenements, formerly butcher's stalls, situate in front of the old Bridewell"'. Possibly a present-day committee might reluctantly decide not to oppose demolition of such well-documented examples of social history if they were in a state of complete decay, but they would be unlikely to write and thank the owner for the *sacrifice* he had made in removing such buildings! What would Mrs Schofield's friends have made of the SPS's strenuous efforts in the 1970s to save Leiston Long Shop or the old station at Newmarket?

Educating Public Opinion

How, then, did the aims and objects of the SPS of those early days compare with those of today? It is perhaps rather surprising to find how enlightened were the

Thornham Magna Post Mill, photographed for the SPS's mill survey about 1936.

Tricker's Mill, Woodbridge. It ceased working in about 1920; the tower can still be seen close to the town centre.

aims and how much was already being done. In 1931, the year before any inhabited buildings came under statutory protection, the SPS was considering compiling its own register of important buildings that it wished to see preserved, and, after the Town and Country Planning Act of 1932, the Society was asked to assist in compiling the list of scheduled buildings. Not everyone was happy about this; Charles Partridge had, in his characteristically forthright manner, warned, at the Society's inception, of the dangers of spoiling objects of interest by too much love. 'Above all,' he is reported to have said, 'don't let us go about scheduling things. There are always sharks following the good ship Archaeology.' As with all lively organizations, there were obviously differences of opinion in the SPS from the start.

The propaganda poster that was designed to attract new members in the early years was the subject of one of these conflicts. It is clear, even from the measured terms of the minutes, that a good deal of argument surrounded both the poster and a suggestion that a 'Fine Arts Committee' of artists and architects should be set up. It was Hilda Mason, herself a distinguished architect, who proposed this, but it seems to have been resented by the members of the poster committee as a reflection on their taste.

Propaganda and education were a vitally important part of the work from the very beginning, and it is depressing to see how both these ideals faded in later years, so that in 1964 the Secretary, Michael Westropp, replying to a questionnaire from the Civic Trust, was obliged to admit that the Society organized no educational courses as it felt that they were 'somewhat outside the scope of the Society'

30

– a very different attitude from that of Mrs Schofield. Her Committee was in constant touch with schools, inviting the senior pupils to lectures and sending lecturers out. It may be that the sometimes rather elderly lecturers misjudged their young audiences; certainly they do not seem to have had much success, judging from the lack of interest shown in Suffolk by the next generation.

It is often assumed that early amenity societies were interested only in the countryside, had no time for towns, and had little appreciation of groups of buildings, reserving their attention for isolated examples of high architectural merit. If this was the case in general, the SPS was an exception. It is true that they had little interest in towns like Felixstowe or Lowestoft (until recently, such towns tended to be neglected by conservationists), but this is understandable. The pleasures of Felixstowe lie mainly in its Edwardian character which, in 1930, had about as much charm for the middle-aged as the architecture of the 1940s has for us today. Buildings of this kind were too close in date: many people would have been able to remember Felixstowe's pleasant streets being built. Even Georgian architecture was treated casually; it was not until 1937 that the Georgian Group was founded as a splinter group of the SPAB to try and stay the heavy hands of local authorities.

Ipswich

Since 1918, Ipswich Corporation had been pursuing a rigorous programme to provide new, less crowded living conditions for the rising population. In that year, plans were made for 1,400 municipal dwellings outside the confines of the

"Well, Walter, I think we've picked *everything*. We must come here again *next* year."

The council estate on the site of the Ipswich racecourse, begun in 1921 to house people removed from the town centre.

Borough. The Town Planning Act 1919 obliged all boroughs or urban districts with populations of over 20,000 to prepare Town Planning Schemes, and in 1921 the Borough Council met to discuss the preparation of a scheme for part of the north-eastern side of the town, extending into the Rural District of Woodbridge. During the early 1920s, houses partly subsidized by the government were built on the fringes of Ipswich, and the estate laid out between the roads leading to Felixstowe and Nacton was the Corporation's showpiece. Many of its streets were proudly named after members of the Borough Council: Ransome Road, Rands

Way, Bantoft Terrace and Badshah Avenue, this last a tribute to the remarkable Kavas Jamas Badshah, who must have been the only Indian to become mayor of an English provincial town in the 1920s. He was an enthusiastic promoter of better housing for the poor and much of the initiative for new council housing undoubtedly came from him.

However much Mrs Schofield and her SPS Committee might have approved of the actions of the Borough Council, they were not happy about the way in which the town centre, where the council tenants had originally lived, was being destroyed. The ancient buildings near St Mary Elms and close to St Helen's Street had certainly reached a Dickensian intensity of squalor hard to imagine today, infested with rats and bugs, without any kind of sanitation, with leaking roofs and rotten floorboards. The practically minded councillors could see no solution but to destroy them completely. The SPS thought otherwise. Perhaps they could persuade the authorities to keep the timber framework of the houses and rebuild the rest? They were the dilapidated, picturesque muddle which gave the town an endearing character that it has now lost. The Housing and Town Planning Committee had no time for such sentiments.

Road widening, with the increasing traffic in the early 1930s, became an important issue in the towns, particularly those like Ipswich, where the narrow streets were unsuitable for two-way motor traffic. In 1931, the demolition of buildings on the south sides of the Butter Market and Tavern Street caused Mrs Schofield to bombard the SPAB with letters complaining against what she termed the 'abominably ornate' style adopted by quite distinguished architects in the town. Her understanding of the authentic East Anglian vernacular, based on the work of Basil Oliver, was outraged by what she saw. 'The general trend of taste,' she complained to A. R. Powys, 'both in our Society and in Ipswich, is for many embellishments on any so-called Tudor work.'

There is no doubt that she felt some sense of betrayal when the representative of the SPAB decided to drop opposition to the demolition of two houses in Tavern Street, on the advice of the Mayor of Ipswich, since it was 'so decidedly against the views of the Corporation'. In the same year, the proposal to demolish three timber-framed houses on St Margaret's Plain caused considerable protest in the pages of the local papers. The owner was anxious to save them from compulsory purchase for road widening, and the SPS, gathering support from the Suffolk Institute of Archaeology as well as many other individuals, again approached the SPAB. Again the representative consulted the Mayor, and the same advice was given. Mrs Schofield wrote despairingly to the SPAB after seeing the plans for the buildings which were to replace those that so many people had fought for. She deplored the 'imitation of ancient work, the frightful erection we shall probably see in time on St Margaret's Plain'. And she complained bitterly of 'a Corporation which loves obsolete trolley-buses more than medieval buildings'.

It is rather hard to understand the attitude of the SPAB towards Ipswich from today's standpoint. Those who remember the town in the 1920s speak with affection of its charm and its intimate human scale. The SPAB was, by the standards of the day, an old-established organization with vast experience in the problems of ancient towns and their buildings, and the Secretary must have had many dealings with borough councils far more philistine than that of Ipswich. It is

What Ipswich has lost. These houses were demolished in the early 1960s, but much of similar quality had gone before the Second World War.

St Margaret's Plain, Ipswich. The SPS fought to save these houses, which were demolished for road widening in 1931.

The result of road widening. The style of these replacements is typical of much rebuilding of Ipswich in the 1930s.

The Ancient House, Ipswich, with the 'Queen Anne style' cinema, once known as the 'Ritz'.

possible that the Secretary felt that the buildings he was being asked to try and save were not of prime architectural importance. He could hardly have felt this when he gave the following report on the proposed cinema to be built beside the Ancient House to Mrs Schofield in August 1931, only a month after the failure over St Margaret's Plain:

> The design for the cinema had been seen by a friend on whose judgement he relied and who reported that it was in the Queen Anne style and would probably be as suitable as was possible for the site next to the Ancient House.

How many people passing the ABC Cinema today would guess that it was in the 'Queen Anne Style' (so suitable for such a purpose) or that anyone could ever have considered it an acceptable building to stand next to the most important house in Ipswich? So much for the judgement of friends.

In spite of frequent setbacks, the SPS carried on with the defence of their county with undimmed enthusiasm. Not only did Mrs Schofield give time to the work, she was also prepared to spend money on saving buildings which caught her eye on her drives round the county. Sun Court at Hadleigh and Clock House Farm, Little Stonham, both late medieval houses of great quality threatened with

Sun Court, Hadleigh, rescued from decay by Mrs Schofield.

demolition, were bought by her and restored by Sydney Schofield, and they received much help and encouragement in their work from the SPAB. She also induced the Forestry Commission to let her buy Woodcock Covert at Barton Mills, which she presented to the Society, and which was at a later stage handed over to West Suffolk County Council and lost in road widening.

But, on the whole, apart from a few irrelevancies and the personal satisfaction that the purchase of individual properties gave, Mrs Schofield and her Committee never lost sight of the larger issues that had begun to appear at the formation of the Society. Horrified by the new sprawl of bungalows and ribbon development at Kesgrave, they made positive proposals to the County Council for the new Woodbridge by-pass. The suggestion that road frontages should remain undeveloped, and new streets of houses be built at right angles to preserve the rural character of the area (for the motorist at least), might not seem an acceptable solution today, but it showed nevertheless that a good deal of thought was given to problems of this kind and the idea was taken up by the authorities.

Crown-post roof at Clock House Farm, Little Stonham.

Trees and Woodland

Alteration of the landscape in north Suffolk, and to a smaller extent near Woodbridge and at Dunwich, was of a different kind. The 1930s saw the planting of
massive conifer plantations, which was to have such a drastic effect on the bare
Breckland landscape and its ecology.

The Forestry Commission, which had been set up in 1919, was concerned with
meeting the national need for timber, the function given to it by Parliament, and
its utilitarian methods of planting were, in 1935, meeting strong opposition from
the Friends of the Lake District over the proposition to plant the wild and desolate
valley of Ennerdale. In East Anglia, in the same year, the SPS, several learned
societies in Suffolk, and the Norfolk Branch of the CPRE, formed a joint committee
to consider similar action, although it was acknowledged that only small areas of
the Breckland could be kept free. The SPS's main concern was that the Icklingham
Belt, that part of the Icknield Way which had once been part of the London Road

Ancient lime coppice at Groton Wood, now saved from decay by proper management.

and stretched from Thetford to Lackford, should be kept clear of planting. With this they were unsuccessful, though the Joint Committee's recommendation that the outer edges of the plantation should be planted with hardwood was adopted in some places, perhaps as an exercise in public relations. (The Northern amenity societies gained an informal agreement that the central mountain area of the Lake District should not be planted, but no statutory responsibility to consider amenities was laid on the Forestry Commission until 1959.)

A good deal of concern had been expressed as early as 1929 about the loss of ancient woodland in Suffolk. In that year alone, Letheringham Old Park was felled and a historic wood at Bradfield St Clare, now thought by some historians to be the place of St Edmund's martyrdom, was partially destroyed. There was an increasing danger from accidental fires started by careless tourists, as an editorial in the *Suffolk Naturalists Society's Transactions* (1929) pointed out:

> One used to rather enjoy the sight of the hoi-polloi out for a day's joy-ride in the country, for the vapid smile and airy hand-wave were at least cheery. Then one did not detect the sloven inwardness that chucks lighted matches athwart dry grass, and strews unsightly papers and bottles along the King's Highway. Just because it is the King's Highway, no penalty can be inflicted we believe. The sole feasible measure is to enlist every Institute in every village to impress the corps of Boy Scouts, who notes the motor's number and reports such filthy practices, worse than spitting on the carpet because more obvious, to both that motor's proprietor and the powers that be – for the sake indeed, of King and Country.

Naturalists no longer write with such stirring illiteracy.

The SPS waged a constant battle against tree-felling. Their policy at that time was the same as that of all well-intentioned people: to *save* wherever possible. Hardly ever do we read of public authorities actually planting any trees; indeed, it was only in the 1970s that many people woke up to the fact that trees, unless properly managed by pollarding or coppicing, have a limited life. The *East Anglian Daily Times* reported Professor G. M. Trevelyan, addressing the SPS's Annual General Meeting in 1937:

> Whenever he had come into Suffolk he had noticed that its beauty largely depended on trees. He was afraid that 100 years hence, or even 50 years, when the present full-grown deciduous trees were mostly felled that Suffolk would be very much less beautiful if they were not replaced, or if they were replaced almost entirely by conifers. He appealed to members to see that deciduous trees were planted.

The members seem to have ignored his call. So, too, did nearly everybody else.

3 Early Planning

By 1932, it was becoming clear that both the towns and the countryside of England needed proper planning if they were not to be overrun by the pressures of industrialism and the motor car. While in Suffolk, a mainly agricultural county, the threats were less severe than in the industrial towns of the North and Midlands, the problem was officially recognized at a remarkably early stage.

The Survey of East Suffolk

Mrs Schofield had attended the 1931 Conference on Regional and Town Planning at Ashridge. So, too, had Cecil Oakes, Clerk of the East Suffolk County Council, who was swiftly invited to join the SPS Committee and who worked closely with the Society until his death in 1959. At this conference they met Professor Patrick Abercrombie, then Professor of Civic Design at the University of Liverpool and the leader in the field of planning in England. He had created the planning scheme for Bath in 1930, and in 1932 was to become engaged in drawing up a similar scheme for Sheffield. It must have been Cecil Oakes, probably backed by Lord Ullswater, the President of the SPS and a member of the County Council, who suggested that a Regional Planning Committee should be formed, and it was the suggestion of the SPS that Professor Abercrombie should supervise planning matters, an idea which was enthusiastically taken up by the County Council.

Thus it was that East Suffolk, a national backwater which took the lead in little else, became, as the SPS proudly recorded, the county to pioneer 'the first joint Board in England established for the purpose of administering a planning scheme in operation'.

As a preliminary step, Abercrombie undertook, with Sydney A. Kelly, a delightful survey of East Suffolk which must have been a revelation to everyone interested in the county.

To those of us used to the dry, jargon-ridden planning documents of today, it is equally a revelation. Beautifully produced, with maps analysing road systems, village greens, population, railways, woodland, it also includes sensitively written descriptions of those places he considered the most important visually, and it contains photographs, not only of idyllically beautiful places, but also of the less agreeable industrial scenery. It was an expensively produced book which could not have had a wide circulation, but it gave a small number of people a clear idea of the beauties and problems of their county. The survey included the whole of East Suffolk, with the exception of the Borough of Ipswich and Stowmarket Urban District, who seem to have held aloof from the scheme.

Efforts to educate public taste, though vigorous, do not seem to have been much more successful. In 1935, Abercrombie, in his outline survey of East Suffolk,

The SPS Committee approved of the simplicity of the Five Bells Inn at Cavendish.

stressed the importance of suitable building materials for different parts of the county.

He mentioned a pamphlet 'which has been issued by this committee in association with the Suffolk Association of Architects and the Suffolk Preservation Society, and represents the informed architectural opinion of East Suffolk'. This, he said, had already been issued and a second edition would follow with an appendix of model plans and elevations and site layouts of typical small Suffolk houses and estates.

Since there do not seem to be any surviving copies of this pamphlet, we cannot judge how these guidelines would accord with present-day ideas of informed architectural opinion. However, we know enough of Mrs Schofield's personal taste, and the experience of the architectural panel on the East Suffolk Regional Planning Committee, to guess that these model plans would have been firmly based on what we now call vernacular architecture. But the influence which this guidance had on the general design of houses of the period can only be judged by the standard of building produced in the 1930s, and there seems to be very little of any distinction. Certainly the SPS Committee found few new houses of which it could approve. The rebuilt Five Bells Inn at Cavendish earned their praise; it seems to have been designed to the specification of Basil Oliver's booklet, *The Modern Public House*.

It is a little sad to think of so much work and enthusiasm going to waste. The hope that builders would respond to persuasion rather than compulsion (though the Planning Committee had no power to compel in any case) was a vain one. However fruitless, though, these guidelines anticipated Essex County Council's *A Design Guide for Residential Areas* by forty-odd years.

Abercrombie's survey suggested that the first step towards accomplishing a realistic plan for East Suffolk should be to appoint a County Planning Officer, and in 1934 Mr T. B. Oxenbury was offered the post. Such an appointment was something of an innovation, and we may be fairly certain that, without a nucleus of interested people in the County Council and an informed group such as the SPS, it would have been some time before the Council would have made such a move. West Suffolk still held aloof and showed no interest in the new idea, but in East Suffolk the whole of the area came under planning control for the first time, with the exception of Stowmarket Urban District.

The hobby of Mr. Binks, the house-agent, is sketching from Nature. It is curious to note how his business influences it.

43

Planning for the Countryside

The 1932 Town and Country Planning Act was the first instance of the *country* being the subject of official recognition. By modern standards, planning regulations were loose; local authorities were encouraged, but not compelled to draw up town planning schemes for small towns. Areas were designated for future development and agricultural land divided into three categories: *temporary*, which was seen as a protection against ribbon development, where single houses or small groups might be allowed; *permanently restricted zones*, where there might be only one house in twenty-five acres; and *prohibited areas*, where the land was completely unsuited to building. This scheme had, as Abercrombie later pointed out, a suburban bias which seemed to put building development before the needs of agriculture. There was little detailed planning. Zones were designated for housing or industry, and there were certain restrictions on the height and size of buildings beyond the suggestions of the Regional Planning Committee. The county council bore the cost of the organization, though it had advisory powers only, and there was little money to spend on major projects.

An Act of 1937 made county councils, for the first time, the statutory planning authority. West Suffolk still seems to have done very little until 1941, when Mr Oxenbury was appointed to supervise planning in both halves of the county. With Miss Elizabeth Chesterton, his Assistant Planning Officer, whose intimate knowledge of Suffolk was put to such good use in later years, he spent much of the war period in working on a survey of the whole county, published in 1945; a work of outstanding excellence and one which was the first stage in the 1950 *Outline Plan for Suffolk*.

4   Changes: 1937–49

In 1937, Mrs Schofield announced her resignation to the Committee. Her husband, anxious for a change of scene for his painting, wished to move to Cornwall, and Mrs Schofield, feeling that her increasing deafness and her lack of typing and driving were hampering her in the growing work of the Society, reluctantly agreed. As Founder and Hon. Secretary of the SPS, she was, as secretaries often are, the prime mover in all the work undertaken, but she left the Society in a sufficiently inspired and healthy state to carry on until the outbreak of war. An indication of her love of Suffolk is contained in a letter from her son Seymour to Francis Engleheart (Chairman, 1956–63) on her death in 1960:

> I think it would be fair to say that my Mother lost her real interest in life when she left Suffolk in 1937, for she was completely absorbed in the work of the Society. When, shortly after the war, she was invited to give an address on the early work of the Society at the Annual General Meeting, I was honorary Secretary, and was rather apprehensive that she would be too old to recollect details of her past labours, but she seemed to have dwelt so much on those days in Suffolk that she was not at all confused.

At intervals during Mrs Schofield's term of office, the question of the Society's relationship with the CPRE had cropped up. Several members of the Committee were anxious that the affiliation of the Society should be strengthened by accepting the CPRE's invitation to become their Suffolk branch, but Mrs Schofield herself was not enthusiastic. She felt that the independence of the Society would be threatened by such an amalgamation. Shortly after her departure, however, the members voted overwhelmingly to become a branch of the CPRE, though the decision was still hotly contested by a few people.

On Mrs Schofield's departure, the Rev. (later Canon) W. M. Lummis took over as Hon. Secretary. Mr Rowley Elliston was still Chairman, and there were 254 members. For the first time, a Treasurer was appointed; previously the job had been combined with that of the Hon. Secretary.

The new Secretary, Mr Lummis, was a dedicated antiquarian, and under his leadership the excursions which the Society had occasionally organized became a regular annual event. The outing to the Nayland area in July 1937 attracted the members' attention to Arger Fen near Bures, which was described as 'a wild patch worthy of preservation'. It was over twenty years before this preservation was achieved by the combined efforts of the Suffolk Naturalists Society, the Nature Conservancy Council and the SPS, by an agreement with the Forestry Commission.

There was no shortage of new ideas. Hilda Mason was anxious that the Society should form a company, run on the lines of the already well-established Cam-

Central Suffolk has been the principal casualty of hedge removal. The hedge lines in this aerial view of a farm in Tannington can be easily identified even without the accompanying map.

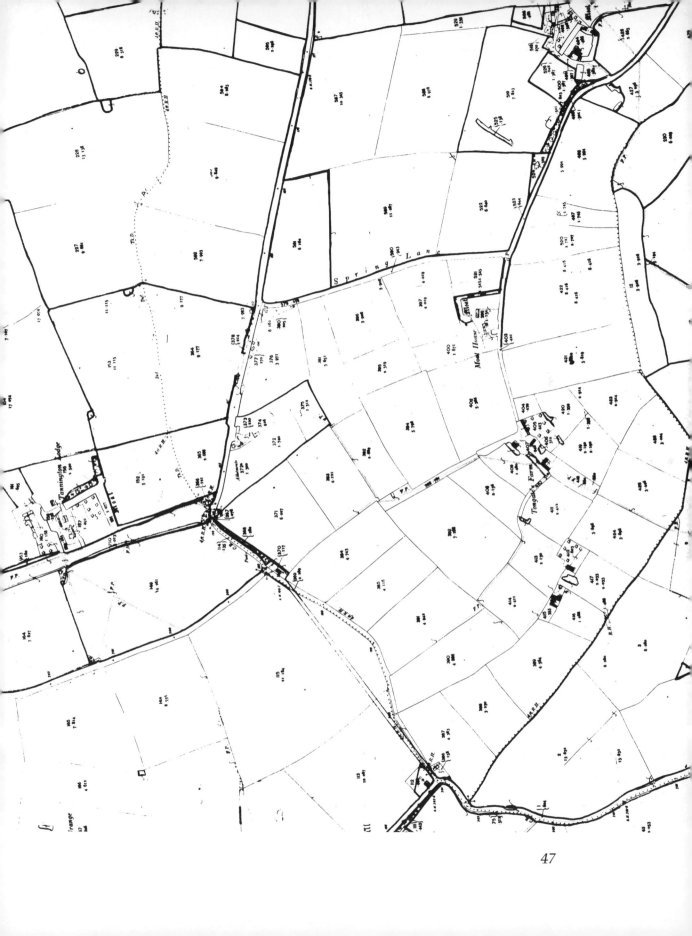

47

bridgeshire Cottage Improvement Society, to buy and restore properties which would otherwise decay or be demolished. Though land and buildings had been offered to the Society on various occasions, legal and practical difficulties had made it necessary to refuse them. Over thirty years later, this idea became a reality with the forming of the Suffolk Building Preservation Trust in 1973.

The SPS had, by 1938, collected about 400 members. A glance at the early membership list shows that most of them were country dwellers and, like the members of most other amenity societies, they appear to have belonged to the middle class. Though, in a county population of about 400,000, they were a small group, they may have formed a larger proportion of the total compared with other amenity bodies. It seems fair to assume that nearly all the members of the Committee were middle-aged and had sufficient leisure to attend day-time meetings, but the Society had, with the excellent publicity provided by the *East Anglian Daily Times*, become an organization which was familiar to the public, and it had become, particularly in East Suffolk, an accepted part of the consultative body for planning schemes.

Since few of the members lived in the towns, it was natural that most of the cases brought to the attention of the Committee concerned the villages and the landscape.

There seems, in those days, to have been no hostility to such aims, no accusations of 'interfering', or the cry of, 'You can't stop progress,' which became so common after the war. The *East Anglian Daily Times* even went so far as to nickname the Society 'Suffolk's Ministry of Amenity', and although the membership was slow in growing, there seems to have been a general acceptance that a preservation society was a good thing and that there was nothing necessarily backward-looking about such an organization.

Suffolk had never had to change direction at the Industrial Revolution in the way that London, the Midlands and Yorkshire had been forced to do. It had remained, on the whole, an agricultural county, its medieval industrial past forgotten. The people who held sway in local government were mainly owners of large estates and gentlemen farmers, with a sprinkling of smaller farmers on the rural district councils. There was little serious threat from industry, and if there had been, it is likely that the farming community would have strongly resisted it. Though there was some increase in the population of the larger villages, it was the towns which began to build out beyond their old boundaries. The sprawl of buildings in the country was only one problem among others which included the job of preserving cottages and preventing an indiscriminate tangle of electricity lines.

Disappearing Hedgerows

The farmers, however, were already affecting the landscape in their own way. In 1939, a letter sent to *The Times* by Guy Winkfield of the Men of the Trees Society, drew attention to the rapid disappearance of hedges and hedgerow trees. In discussing the matter, the SPS Committee deplored the destruction of hedgerows mainly from the point of view of their picturesqueness, no mention being made of their contribution to the wild-life population, or of their historical significance, though the Chairman said that he had always considered there to be 'something in the old theory that hedges contributed to the formation of humus'! There was a sharp division of opinion among the Committee about the usefulness of hedges, and there seems to have been no attempt to make any constructive move.

At this same meeting came the first mention of the allied topic which continues to distress conservationists today: that of 'prairie farming'. Threats of war were in the air, and the development of mechanized farming methods and the need for an

MRS. HAWKINS. " 'Ave a good look round, Bert, and see that we 'aven't left anythink."

Bungay Castle. In spite of the efforts of local people, this ancient monument was not officially scheduled until 1960.

increase in home-produced food gave farmers every excuse for ripping out as many hedges as they could. Indeed, agricultural institutes were advocating their removal to get the sun and air to the fields. In a county like Suffolk, where the central two-thirds had been enclosed from medieval times, the loss of the small ancient field boundaries made a dramatically altered picture, but, in the face of such pressure from the professionals, little could be done except to express concern in the pages of the minute book.

English people being what they are, it would have taken more than the sinister moves of Nazi Germany to deter them from carrying on in a normal way in the uneasy peace of 1938–9. In this period another, smaller, but none the less influential amenity group was set up: the Dedham Vale Society – a more particularly *preservationist* group, and rightly so, intent on keeping the Constable Country on both sides of the Stour as completely unchanged as was possible in the modern world. This Society, though originating in Essex, formed strong links with the SPS.

Wartime

Despite the growing difficulty of influencing the ever-increasing official bodies who dictated inflexible policies as war drew nearer, the SPS appear to have continued as if nothing were happening. True, one of the early committee members quietly disappeared, having been interned as a member of the British Union of Fascists, but little mention is made in the minutes of any impending national calamity, beyond the rather curious choice of Bungay Castle as a possible air-raid shelter. Here the Committee's concern echoed that of the Town Reeve of Bungay, who had strenuously pressed, without success, for some kind of scheduling for the great twelfth-century keep. A glance at those familiar case-histories reveals nothing that might not have happened ten years before: flooding at Flatford, Cavendish Church cottages, windmills (for which the advice of Rex Wailes, a leading expert, had been enlisted) and, as ever, Lavenham. Again and again the spreading of electricity wires and pylons comes to the fore, but there is nothing to foreshadow the events which were to suspend for several years all that had already been planned, and which were to bring important changes: the army camps, the prisoner-of-war camps and, above all, the airfields that were to disfigure the Suffolk scene. Only the lack of entries about planning schemes indicates that there was anything in the wind.

With the coming of the war, and the interruption of the whole pattern of development in England, the SPS suffered a serious setback. At such a time it was impossible for the authorities to pay much attention to people concerned with the preservation of the countryside, when the preservation of the entire nation was at stake. Basic essentials had to come first. Who could resist the ploughing up of ancient heathland to provide more food for a country which had to learn to be self-sufficient? Who could protest about the large numbers of new airfields in a county that had such easy access to the Continent and stretches of flat land suitable for landing strips?

As so often happens, the threat of destruction awakens an appreciation of things taken for granted. The war period produced a profusion of surveys to record what might be lost by enemy action. In 1941, the Royal Commission on Historical Monuments, alert to the possibility of losing many important buildings, set up the National Buildings Record, now incorporated in the National Monuments Record, and the SPS nominated Canon Lummis as its representative. It was on his initiative that the incumbents of all Suffolk churches were asked to produce details of their buildings, though a copy of Munro Cautley's *Suffolk Churches and their Treasures*, first issued in 1938, might have been a more reliable guide. The National Trust, in 1943, commissioned Hilda Mason to make a landscape survey; it was to pinpoint outstanding areas which might be purchased by the Trust, and though the SPS Committee made some suggestions none was taken up.

Lavenham

But it was Cosford Rural District Council which took the most far-sighted initiative in commissioning the joint report on Lavenham which, in 1944, pre-dated by five years the first of the town surveys produced by the East and West Suffolk County Councils. The RDC called in Marshall Sisson, representing the Suffolk Preservation Society, and John McGregor for the SPAB, to prepare a detailed plan. This seems to have been an innovation; there had been few surveys of big cities at this time, let alone of small towns, even those of such outstanding interest as Lavenham, but it seems likely that Cosford took notice of a certain agitation on the part of Lavenham residents, who were concerned at the lack of control over unsuitable alterations to their historic buildings. (It was not the first time Lavenham people had taken the lead, as we have seen.)

McGregor and Sisson's report recommended that there should be some sort of society or group to monitor developments in Lavenham, and they undoubtedly knew that such a group was in the process of forming since their meetings with Cosford councillors had been at Little Hall, the house of notable twin brothers, Major R. G. Gayer-Anderson and Colonel T. G. Gayer-Anderson.

The Gayer-Anderson Brothers

The brothers had made Lavenham their permanent English base in 1924. Both had had eventful careers in the army, particularly in Egypt where Major Gayer-Anderson later spent his retirement until 1942. Before he left Cairo, he was given the title of 'Pasha' by King Farouk, and he handed over a sixteenth-century Arab house and its contents as the Gayer-Anderson Pasha Museum of Oriental Arts and Crafts. Both brothers were avid collectors of oriental works of art, and the 'Pasha' presented a valuable collection to the Fitzwilliam Museum at Cambridge.

Of the two, it was Colonel T. G. Gayer-Anderson who spent more time at Lavenham. The Great House in the Market Place and the adjoining building, divided up as cottages, were found as the brothers went on a clockwise journey covering a sixty-mile radius round London to search for a house. The entire block of buildings was then covered with a cement and pebble layer – 'slopdash', as it was called locally – and, on the advice of A. R. Powys of the SPAB, the outer coating was stripped off the cottage end. Mr Powys found that this part was in fact all one house and identified it as having originally been a fifteenth-century house

Little Hall, Lavenham. The home of the Gayer-Anderson brothers, now the headquarters of the Suffolk Preservation Society.

with an open hall, probably belonging to a Lavenham clothier. The Gayer-Andersons, having first lived in the Great House, refurbished the older house and, in 1932, sold the Great House to the poet Stephen Spender before moving into what they now called Little Hall.

Colonel Gayer-Anderson was a good deal more enthusiastic about Lavenham than his brother. We tend to forget, in our romantic enthusiasm for the English countryside, how much main drainage and removal of rotting timbers and damp walls have contributed to our feelings about the healthy country life. The Major, in his unpublished memoirs, remembered Lavenham with little affection:

> From the very start I felt that there was something unlovely, sinister, evil about it and its inhabitants. . . . I took practically no part in its life and affairs, I could not help hearing of them and sensing that strange morbid and ugly side. . . .

As late as the mid-1950s, the impression made on anyone seeing Lavenham for the first time could have been very similar; there *was* a sense of decay, almost of decadence about it even then, though by that time there must have been many improvements. How quickly the atmosphere of a place can change! Nowadays the town is almost too well kept, too clean, too pretty to have the slightest air of mystery about it, and there is certainly nothing remotely sinister about its inhabitants.

The Lavenham Preservation Committee

Together with the Rector, the Rev. Martin Fountain Page, and Mr Lingard Ranson, the most dedicated of Lavenham preservationists, the Gayer-Andersons formed the Lavenham Preservation Committee. Colonel Gayer-Anderson was quite clear as to the need for such a body. The Parish Council, he suggested,

> . . . is naturally enough, in the case of so unique a town as Lavenham, not artistically or creatively-minded enough as a body to deal adequately with important artistic problems which may arise.

Though it was for such aesthetic questions that the Committee was formed, it quickly found itself in the forefront of a major row. Cosford RDC, recognizing that there would be a need for new housing at the end of the war, put forward plans to build fifty council houses on Pit Meadow to the south-west of the town. As a result of the storm of protest, a public meeting was held which became 'very heated', and Sir Alfred Munnings accused the RDC of spoiling the ancient amenities of Lavenham.

As far as the Lavenham Preservation Committee was concerned, there was no denying that there was a need for new housing. The strong feeling was against extending the building over open fields and the isolation of the community from the rest of the town. Colonel Gayer-Anderson pointed out that there were plenty of sites in Old Lavenham where pairs or small groups of houses could be built. There were already, he said, more than 130 small nineteenth- and twentieth-century houses built cheek by jowl with Tudor cottages, and plenty of those cottages could be reconditioned 'if vested rights could be overruled'.

McGregor and Sisson's report, while covering the question of this kind of rebuilding and reconditioning, recommended Pit Meadow as the most suitable site, since it provided ample space for building in the future, was well placed for drainage and water supplies and, above all, would make little impression on the general picture of Lavenham.

Faced with the inevitable, Colonel Gayer-Anderson, though obviously disappointed, set to work with touching enthusiasm on a layout for the new estate which would make, as he saw it, the best of a bad job. Not only that, but he also drew up plans for 'The Lavenham House', including a number of carefully thought out features for the convenience of the tenants. The site was to include a small block of flats, a sports pavilion, a recreation centre, restaurant and open-air swimming pool. He also prudently suggested an area where future building might take place, but it was the central open green, the recreation ground and children's play area that he was most attached to. The Council did adopt the layout in principle: a dull one by any standards, but it at least had the merit of spaciousness.

It must be remembered that in 1944 the definitive listing of buildings of historic interest was in its infancy and that there was no legal protection of a building even of the importance of the Lavenham Guildhall, nor any official recognition of what we now call 'group value' or, as the joint report put it, a number of other buildings 'not intrinsically remarkable but satisfactory in scale that are valuable in carrying on the line of the street frontage'. The surveyors considered such buildings worthy of careful and sympathetic consideration and that their preservation was most desirable in order to retain the unique character of the town. The report was the first example in Suffolk of an appreciation of a town as a whole, rather than of its individual buildings. It included a map and schedule of everything considered worthy of preservation, and suggested that the Lavenham Preservation Committee should have on it a representative of the Parish Council and should, in conjunction with the SPAB and SPS, advise and co-operate with the Council on all matters concerning the preservation of the beauty and amenity of Lavenham.

The Lavenham Preservation Committee's position was consolidated by this report, and in the following year the Committee approached Sir Cuthbert Quilter, asking him if he would present the Guildhall to the town. After two years of negotiation, it was handed over, and later conveyed to the National Trust.

Although isolated improvements took place in the 1940s, many of Lavenham's buildings were decaying fast. The *Sunday Chronicle* announced, in 1949, with a dramatic picture of crumbling houses, 'Picture Postcard Town is Slum'. But help was on the way, though not necessarily the kind of help that everyone wanted.

To a certain extent, places like Lavenham had been a haven for the retired gentry for some years. Now, in the early 1950s, with the increased mobility that the war had stifled and the quest for somewhere quieter, less populated and above all cheaper, the retired middle class and a certain number of painters and writers – those people not necessarily tied to London – began to filter into Suffolk. Lavenham was an obvious target. House prices were far lower than in the Home Counties, and in this period many of Lavenham's medieval houses were taken over and restored by the newcomers, some more successfully than others. The influx, though a godsend in that it saved much that might have decayed altogether, did nothing to bring the town to life. It was a town where a child or a young person was a rarity; a town for the tourist to come and marvel at on summer week-ends. What youth there was was confined to the council houses on Pit Meadow (how much more satisfactory would have been the integration of council tenants into the old town), and what was happening there? The Council was proposing to build twenty semi-detached bungalows on the central green – just as Colonel Gayer-Anderson had feared; his suggested sites for extension were too expensive to be procured.

The Lavenham Preservation Committee was torn in half. Two of its members, also members of the Parish Council, had voted for the bungalows to be built on the green. Colonel Gayer-Anderson resigned from the chairmanship in disgust. A public inquiry was called, at which he and a good many other residents and organizations protested, but in vain. To see the Pit Meadow development today is to look on an idealistic experiment which failed.

'Alderman and an Old Figurehead'. The Evening Star and Daily Herald, 5 June 1939: '"Nearly Indecent": Owner says "Beautiful"' – a minor battle at Southwold.

56

5 Decline and Revival

By the end of the war there had been a considerable falling off in the work of the Suffolk Preservation Society. Meetings had dwindled. In 1940, when Viscount Ullswater resigned as President and was succeeded by Sir John Tilley, they were held every two months, but, as the war progressed, only a few meetings were held and Canon Lummis was forced, through lack of help, to deal alone with most of the cases which still flowed in with surprising frequency.

The CPRE called frequent war-time meetings to discuss their policy for the return to normality after the war, for there would certainly be a great deal of patching up to be done in the countryside. Though little of Suffolk, apart from Lowestoft, suffered really serious damage, airfields and army camps had to be tidied up and in some cases reclaimed, and a number of larger houses had been battered by the rough treatment of billeted soldiers.

The effects of the war were slow to disappear. There was even an intensification of land use for military training, which greatly concerned the SPS. There had been thirty-four wartime airfields (of which sixteen were USAF bases), and the Air Ministry retained a firm hold on nearly all of them. Vast tracts of agricultural land had been taken over and the airfields had become obtrusive features in the landscape. There are traces of many of them still; often, on a peaceful excursion, one may find stark concrete runways sandwiched between fields of corn. The problems posed by *disuse* of military areas were almost as difficult to solve as the danger and inconvenience to the public of those still in use, and although today we may regard a pillbox as an interesting historic monument which should be preserved, there were large numbers of army huts and coastal gun emplacements which nobody wanted but nobody would remove. Noise, too, was a nuisance that people had been prepared to put up with in wartime, but country residents felt they had a right to return to the former peace and quiet of days undisturbed by large numbers of aeroplanes. The post-war increase of air and road traffic made it harder and harder to find a quiet spot.

Tourism

Though Suffolk had had its share of visitors in pre-war years – the cyclists and the motorists, none of whom were particularly welcomed by anyone except the tea-shop proprietors – little attempt had been made to promote it as a tourist area. The seaside resorts, genteel Felixstowe or old-fashioned Southwold, it is true, provided for summer visitors, but inland those honeypots for the modern tourist, Lavenham, Kersey or Flatford Mill, were unknown except to the locals or to a perceptive traveller like Julian Tennyson, whose *Suffolk Scene* (1939) describes a secret, innocent and unselfconscious countryside which seems a hundred years removed in time from us, rather than a mere forty.

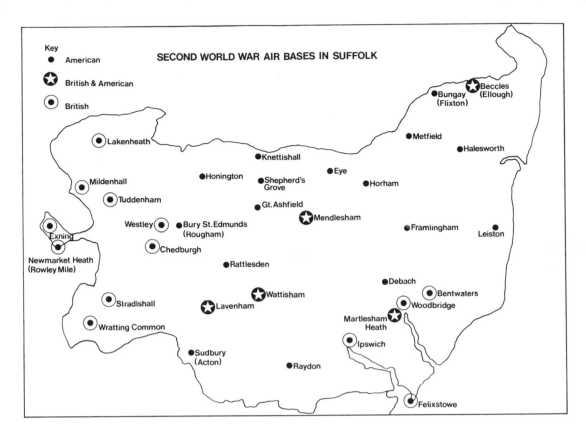

Key
- American
- British & American
- British

SECOND WORLD WAR AIR BASES IN SUFFOLK

- Beccles (Ellough)
- Bungay (Flixton)
- Metfield
- Halesworth
- Lakenheath
- Knettishall
- Eye
- Honington
- Shepherd's Grove
- Horham
- Mildenhall
- Tuddenham
- Gt. Ashfield
- Mendlesham
- Westley
- Bury St. Edmunds (Rougham)
- Framlingham
- Leiston
- Exning
- Chedburgh
- Newmarket Heath (Rowley Mile)
- Rattlesden
- Debach
- Bentwaters
- Wattisham
- Woodbridge
- Stradishall
- Lavenham
- Martlesham Heath
- Wratting Common
- Ipswich
- Sudbury (Acton)
- Raydon
- Felixstowe

Sir Ronald Storrs, at the first AGM after the war, was one of the first to recognize that the promotion of the English countryside as a tourist attraction was on its way, though had he been able to foresee the results of such promotion, he might have been less enthusiastic.

Every day we open the newspapers to receive the warning that we are in for an austerer form of living because of the necessity of exports. I suggest that the English countryside is one of our greatest invisible exports because it will attract more and more people of other nations who have more money to spend on travel than we have. It is our duty to help our country to get more money into it by preserving the beauties and amenities of the countryside.

Taken out of context, this passage looks like an attempt at cynical exploitation of natural beauty, but to his audience it probably seemed a judicious blend of national pride and plain common sense.

The Need for Change

Alongside this growing realization that Suffolk's beauty had an economic as well as an aesthetic value, the SPS was becoming conscious of new developments, political and social, which were to call for a much more comprehensive understanding of planning for the future than had been necessary in the pre-war era. Then, the main concerns had been to protect individual buildings and small areas of land, and to try and educate a not unwilling public into a better understanding of its environment. During the war, the County Planning Officer had conducted a survey of the whole county, this time, unlike the Abercrombie survey, taking in West Suffolk as well. The interim report on the *Outline Plan* appeared in 1950, by which time the possibility that the next two decades would bring a huge increase in the population of Britain had been realized. As early as 1946, mention was being made in the SPS minutes of the promotion of New Towns which the Committee suggested might be accommodated on some of the disused airfields.

This was a period when the SPS, had it been properly prepared, might have exerted a really formative influence on the future of Suffolk, but it missed its chance. It is not hard to see why. The Chairman, Mr Rowley Elliston, whose scholarship and enthusiasm had contributed greatly to the Society, was an old man; Canon Lummis, who had done so much to keep alive the spirit that Mrs Schofield had injected into the Society, was beginning to find the demands of the secretaryship impossible to combine with his pastoral duties, and had to resign. The Committee still contained many able people, but the majority of them were elderly and had neither the time nor the inclination to reconsider and reform the Society to keep pace with the complex new procedures of planning and new social pressures. The membership was dwindling, many of the original members having died. No fresh attempt was made to recruit younger people, and there was no active involvement required of them. But though nothing very constructive was done to fit Suffolk for its new life in the post-war world, many smaller triumphs were achieved under the secretaryship of Seymour Schofield, the son of the Founder. In fairness, it must be said that there was probably a strong body of opinion on the Committee that it was no part of the Society's function to try and influence the county councils in their planning for the future. These people might have been surprised by the participation of the Society in later years in the preparation of town surveys and development plans.

Windmills

Relations with the two county councils were excellent. SPS representatives attended all meetings of both planning committees, and there were plenty of opportunities for conservationist views to be aired. In West Suffolk, the SPS took the lead in advocating the placing of electricity cables underground in Kersey; and, in East Suffolk, the SPS's suggestion that the Council should preserve at least one windmill of each type resulted in the purchase and restoration by the Council of Herringfleet smock mill, and of Buttrum's tower mill at Woodbridge, with considerable help from public appeals and the Pilgrim Trust, and the purchase of Saxtead post mill by the Ministry of Works.

But the windmills were falling fast in spite of energetic efforts by local people to save many of them. Water mills were largely disregarded or being turned to other uses. Flatford Mill had become the world's first Field Studies Council Centre, many others had been gutted and reconstructed as dwelling houses, and those still working were rapidly falling into disrepair. The SPS was called on again and

again by enthusiasts who did not wish to lose their local mills. Little could be done, for the Society had very limited funds. Apart from subscriptions, which remained, despite frequent attempts to raise them, at five shillings until 1964, the Society had only £100 given by Mrs Schofield, and £200 which had been handed over to the Society by the defunct Stour Navigation (Trust) Company in 1937 and was earmarked for the preservation of amenities in the Stour valley. All the SPS could do was to suggest ways of raising money and to hand over a few pounds to get repair funds started. The sixty-two windmills recorded by Norman Collinson in 1938 had, in ten years, shrunk to a handful. It was not until 1977 that a few enthusiasts founded the Suffolk Mills Group to organize visits, lectures and working parties.

Seymour Schofield resigned from the secretaryship in 1950, and since he had also been acting as Treasurer, his departure left a big gap in the SPS's organization. Mr F. Bridgeman, Personal Assistant to the Clerk to the East Suffolk County Council, took over as Secretary, and it is a measure of the co-operation that existed between the County and the Society that all the secretarial work, letters, agendas and minutes were typed and duplicated from then on by East Suffolk County Council staff. The time had not yet come for the SPS to be seen as a group which might take a more independent line from the County Council. Other permanent officers were difficult to find, and though two or three dedicated but over-busy people helped with the finances, it was almost inevitable that membership should decline still further, and there was a distinct sense that, though the Committee might feel themselves as busy as ever, there was little or no communication with the members.

Challenges

In 1950, East Suffolk produced its *Outline Plan*, the next step from the survey of 1945, as well as a much-needed *Outline Plan for Lowestoft*, still trying to pick itself up from war damage. *Bury St Edmunds Town Plan*, in the same year, provided for the growth of the population from 17,000 to 25,000. A preliminary study of Woodbridge, in the following year, marked the beginning of East Suffolk's interest in its small historic towns. The SPS left participation in this survey to the re-formed Woodbridge Society, which was founded shortly before the war and can probably claim to be the first local Suffolk amenity society. Much could have been done by the SPS in participating in these early surveys if there had been enough people with sufficient foresight and opportunity to make their views heard, but, in the vitally important years of the 1950s, when so many new challenges arose, it seems as though people were too tired or felt too powerless to try and shape the development of their country.

How astonishing to read that, in 1953, Charles Partridge was quite seriously suggesting that perhaps, in view of the work being done by the County Planning Committees, there was no longer any need for amenity societies! This was in January. In the following November an ominous heading appears in the minutes:

Movement of People from London to Suffolk

Fortunately, not everyone was as optimistic as Mr Partridge, and steps to revitalize the Society were at hand.

The death of Mr Rowley Elliston in 1953 gave the Committee the added impetus to find someone prepared to show a positive lead in coming to terms with new developments, and they found in the Lord Lieutenant of Suffolk, Lord Stradbroke, a man with the vitality and outspokenness to put the Society back on its feet. He became President and, for three years, acted as Chairman as well, until a suitable candidate could be found to take over. Meetings were called to revise the constitution and the functions of the Committee. This still consisted, as for some time past, of the rather unwieldy Council, comprising the thirty regional correspondents, newly appointed, as well as seventeen or so executive committee members. The list of vice-presidents grew to thirty-three, to the disappointment of some, who would have liked to have seen it scrapped altogether.

The work of the Society continued without many dramatic cases for the next three years. There was a good deal of talk, by both county councils, of road improvements, which caused a flutter of concern in various villages, but little was done – merely some cautious and uncontroversial widening. Road traffic, with the railways still working efficiently, had not yet become intolerable, and the authorities were simply trying to plan for the future. Coaches bringing people from Clacton for a 'mystery tour' to Lavenham or East Bergholt had, it is true, begun to cause mild congestion, but Suffolk was still fairly unknown except to those who lived there. But more important issues were looming: as well as talk of overspill, the Government were making plans for atomic power stations, and Suffolk was high on the list for a suitable coastal site. It seemed vital, therefore, that the SPS should be sufficiently strong and well-informed, with officers who were able to devote a good deal of time to the Society's business and who were able to comment intelligently on these proposals. Accordingly, though Lord Stradbroke remained as the active President, a new Chairman and Secretary were found.

Revival

The Chairman was Francis Engleheart, a descendant of the eighteenth-century miniaturist, and a man with strong Suffolk connections. He was a poet and a man deeply sensitive to visual impressions: he is reputed to have fallen into poetic day-dreams when committee discussions bored him (in those days meetings took up only the afternoons – what epics he might have composed during the day-long sessions of today!), but none the less he was an extraordinarily vigorous Chairman. His romantic nature did not prevent him from filing every letter on SPS business and recording the substance of every phone call he ever made. It is true that he seems to have had an artistic vagueness about remembering people's faces, for he had the endearing habit of scribbling short descriptions by the names on the minutes: 'tall, dark; moustache – rather full faced – stout, with briefcase, etc.' Under his chairmanship, the SPS took on a more businesslike aspect. The new Secretary, F. G. M. Westropp, tackled both the massive amount of correspondence and the thankless task of tracking down lapsed members. At his first attempt he could rouse only eighty past members and was subjected to a good deal of unmerited criticism from others.

> You need money and new members [wrote one, rather crustily] and yet nobody apparently could be found 'for several years' to collect subscriptions and retain the members you already have. I hope you will excuse my bluntness. The easiest course would have been for me to ignore your letter, but I should like to support you, providing I am assured that the administration now is more alive than it appeared to have been in the past.

Poor Mr Westropp – he had only just joined the Society himself. His efforts were rewarded by a new influx of two hundred members. Other suggestions, advertising (something that never seems to have found favour, except with Mrs Schofield), reduced subscriptions for husband and wife, and the production of a brochure explaining the aims of the Society, were all brought up, the last two successfully. The brochure, illustrated by Cavendish Morton, the Vice-Chairman, was produced with the aid of a grant from the Civic Trust. Two thousand copies were printed with a map as well as illustrations, at a cost of thirty pounds!

Gainsborough's House

Cavendish Morton played a leading part in the saving of Gainsborough's House, the birthplace of the painter, at Sudbury. Looking at this delightful house today, with the thriving exhibition galleries, it seems incredible that this small cultural centre could ever have been threatened with demolition. An appeal was launched in 1957 to buy the house and hand it over to the National Trust with an endowment. There was a real danger that the sum needed, £5,250, could not be found.

Gainsborough's House, Sudbury.

Cavendish Church Cottages.

The SPS besides contributing £100, sent a letter to the Mayor of Sudbury expressing the anxiety of the Society, and perhaps more pertinently, 'pointing out the financial advantages to the town from such an attraction'.

The money for Gainsborough's House came from the Stour Valley Fund, which was further eaten into for another worthy cause, this time the now famous cottages at Cavendish, which the Cavendish Preservation Society, with the George Savage Trust, were fighting to save. It is difficult to imagine Cavendish without them, yet at that time they were considered, by many residents and local councillors, not worth bothering about. Once they had been restored, they were valued by the community. The fire which later destroyed them came almost as a lesson to those who had not cared for them before, and it would have been hard to find anyone against their rebuilding.

Atomic Power

In 1958, a conference of interested parties, at which the Society was represented, was called at County Hall, Ipswich, to discuss a matter of great importance: the location of atomic power stations. Mr G. C. Lightfoot, who had succeeded Sir Cecil Oakes both as Clerk of East Suffolk County Council and as a member of the SPS Council, gave that body a summary of the work of this conference, and explained what was required in the siting:

1. Proximity to unlimited water supply.
2. Solid ground suitable for heavy foundations.
3. Remoteness from major centres of population.

He explained that underground power lines were out of the question on grounds of cost, and that the lines would consist of pylons 130 feet high spaced at five to the mile. The SPS Committee's choice of the possible sites was: Erwarton Ness, Sizewell and Boyton – though it reserved the right to change its recommendations when more information about the routes of the power lines was available. The most acceptable site, from the Central Electricity Board's point of view, was soon found to be Sizewell, and it was certainly the most remote from heavily populated areas, but the county planners were perturbed by the fact that little thought had been given to the placing of the power lines which would straddle the county on the way to Bedfordshire. The pylons would be twice as high as any previously seen in England, anything between 130 and 180 feet (depending on the contours of the land and the height required), and there would be a double line as far as Needham Market, carrying, as at first thought, 275 kV, which was later increased to 400 kV. Inevitably, the first suggestion from the SPS and others distressed by the damage to the landscape, was that the lines should be put underground, but the appalling costs (£936,000 a mile compared with £50,000) made it clear that there was no hope of achieving such a solution.

By 1961, two alternative routes for the pylon lines had been made public, and the Planning Committees of East and West Suffolk began to consider their attitudes to them. The southern route through West Suffolk followed the existing line of smaller pylons and was much favoured by the planners (it was much shorter than the northern route), but Francis Engleheart's Committee was utterly opposed to the idea, stating, firmly and clear-sightedly, that two differing sizes of pylon along the same route were infinitely more disfiguring than two completely separate lines, though the carrot was held out to them, mistakenly as it proved, that both sets of wires might eventually be hung on the same tower. The SPS was very concerned that this route crossed the valleys of the Stour, Box and Brett, already encumbered with the existing 132 kV line, and that it would be clearly visible in some of the views made famous by Constable.

The Pylon Route

This case was by far the most testing that the SPS had ever had to handle, but they grasped the nettle with courage and expertise and began to plan their own constructive suggestions for a more acceptable route which would pass through country that they felt was less visually interesting than either of the Central Electricity Generating Board's proposals. It was to keep to the line generally favoured in East Suffolk, but to strike across through Whatfield and the Walding-

Pylons. An intrusion or a majestic feature in the landscape?

fields to Rodbridge and into Essex. Michael Westropp conferred with the CPRE and its Essex Branch and the Hertfordshire Society, who all concurred with the SPS's opposition and supported the new route. A folder of photographs of the views which the SPS line would cross was compiled, and the Secretary wrote formally to the Ministry of Housing and Local Government requesting the opportunity of presenting the Society's case at the Public Inquiry.

Public Inquiry

Though this was not the first time the Society had been represented at an inquiry (as far back as 1939 two members had opposed possible ribbon development on the proposed Stratford St Mary by-pass), as the date drew nearer, the importance of the issue and the possibility of very formidable opposition seemed to show that the case needed professional guidance. Thus the services of a QC were obtained, at considerable cost. Much of the expense was borne by the members themselves, for the Society has always been fortunate in having a few members who have been constant and self-effacing benefactors.

As the time for the inquiry approached, the brief to Counsel to appear on behalf of the Society was drawn up, and Michael Westropp prepared his own lengthy and well-reasoned evidence. The inquiry was in two parts, the first on 6 February 1962 at Hertford, which the Secretary and another member attended, and the second at Ipswich on 22 February. At Hertford, beside seventy private objectors, mainly farmers, some of whom already suffered inconvenience from the smaller existing pylons, were the county councils of Hertfordshire, Essex, Bedfordshire and Cambridge, as well as various rural and urban councils. One of the objectors told the inquiry that the pylons would be as high as Nelson's Column, and rightly dismissed the idea that putting them among trees would be of the slightest use. 'They will be like Gulliver in Lilliput among the trees. The trees will be made to look ridiculous.' Throughout the inquiry the SPS confined its evidence to the effects of the pylons on the landscape and expressed no opinion on the use of nuclear power as a national issue.

The case was, of course, lost, as the objectors had probably known it would be. The SPS's careful work was put in the archives and the Chairman could only console himself with the thought that the new monsters had a certain grandeur. Indeed one lady, near Pettistree, who complained bitterly when a pylon was being erected next to her garden, was told by a hurt workman that, 'We think they are rather beautiful.' From that moment on, she confessed that she began to think they were; maybe the twenty-first century may treasure them in much the same way as we now cling to our old railway stations. Meanwhile it seems almost inevitable that the Society will be involved in further controversies over the siting of nuclear plant.

The Dedham Vale Society and the National Trust, with SPS support, had more success in securing the diversion of the subsidiary line planned to run from Ipswich to Colchester, which would have been clearly visible from parts of Constable Country. It proved possible to lay the smaller 132 kV line underground for the short stretch from Manningtree Station to Lawford, where otherwise it would have made the greatest impact.

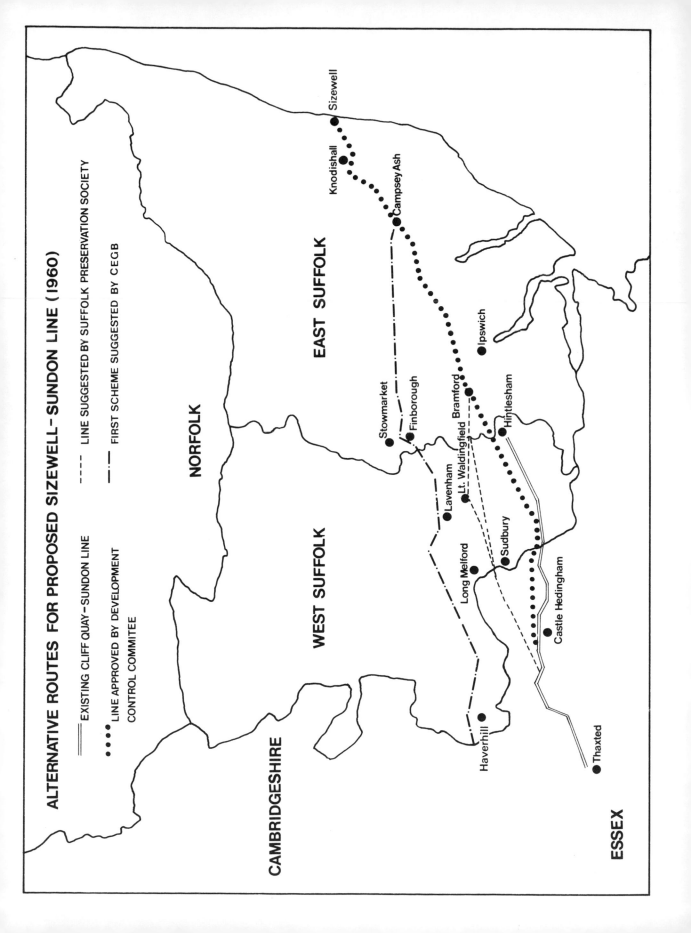

ALTERNATIVE ROUTES FOR PROPOSED SIZEWELL–SUNDON LINE (1960)

— EXISTING CLIFF QUAY–SUNDON LINE

- - - LINE SUGGESTED BY SUFFOLK PRESERVATION SOCIETY

–·–·– FIRST SCHEME SUGGESTED BY CEGB

•••• LINE APPROVED BY DEVELOPMENT
CONTROL COMMITEE

CAMBRIDGESHIRE

NORFOLK

WEST SUFFOLK

EAST SUFFOLK

ESSEX

Sizewell
Knodishall
Campsey Ash
Stowmarket
Finborough
Ipswich
Bramford
Lavenham
Lt. Waldingfield
Hintlesham
Long Melford
Sudbury
Castle Hedingham
Haverhill
Thaxted

Overspill

At the same time as the Committee were wrestling with the Sizewell problem, another issue, which had been first noticed eight years before, was occupying the attention of the SPS. Overspill: that ugly word which heralded an ugly expansion of towns like Haverhill and threatened in some cases to double the population of small towns. In 1955, West Suffolk County Council and Haverhill Urban District Council had spent £455,000 in capital outlay for a scheme which had brought 5,000 Londoners to the town. This was only the beginning. By 1961, West Suffolk had entered into an agreement with the London County Council to import a total of 40,000, the whole scheme to be accomplished in twenty years.

In 1943, the *County of London Plan* had recommended the decentralization of several thousand people, and was followed by the *Greater London Plan*, designed to cope with the outward movement of six or seven hundred thousands. New towns were to be built beyond the ten-mile Green Belt which was then envisaged. The Government's 1952 Town Development Act had made provisions for overspill agreements. West Suffolk had taken up the idea with enthusiasm, partly as a means, as it was then thought, of revitalizing towns such as Bury St Edmunds and Sudbury with industry which might be expected to offset the reduction in agricultural jobs by bringing work for the young people in these towns, and partly, there is no doubt, with a real sense of shouldering the responsibility of the nation's problems.

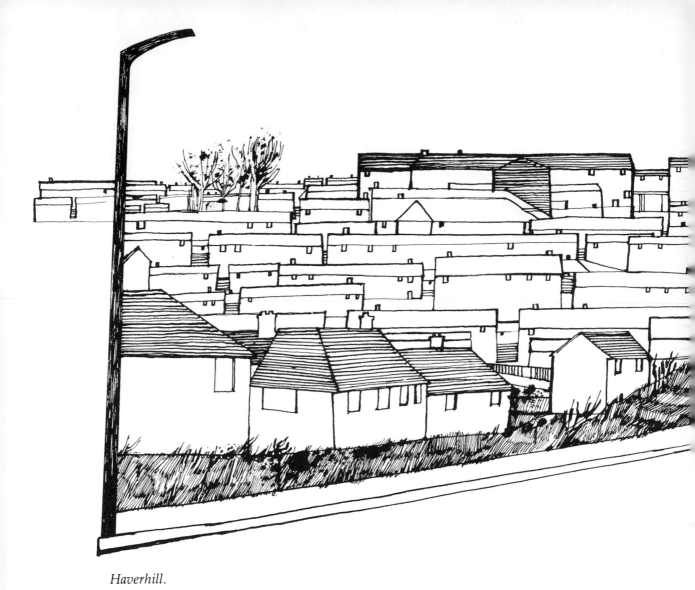

Haverhill.

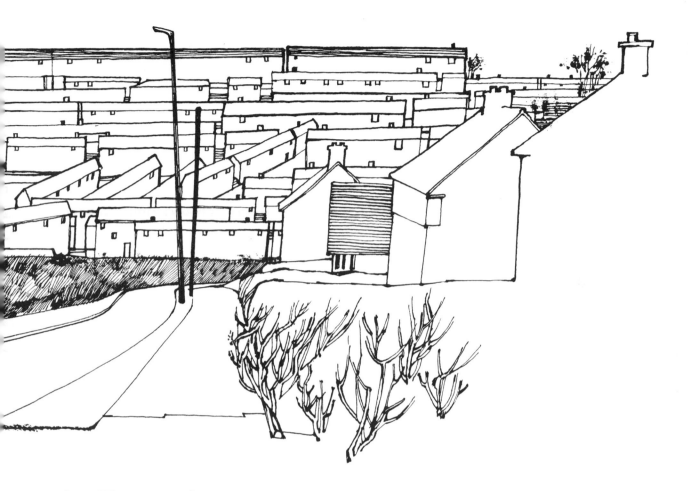

6 Expansion

The West Suffolk County Planning Committee may have been somewhat misled when they made the recommendation to the County Council to enter into the agreement with the LCC described in the previous chapter. They were told that overspill was inevitable, that the Government might well take powers to impose such schemes. In the event, these powers were only assumed by the Labour Government of 1965. There were no more than two dissenting voices out of the twenty members of the Planning Committee which met on 13 July 1961. In less than three weeks, the proposals had been confirmed by a large majority of the County Council, in spite of a letter from the Council of the SPS which emphasized that the problem of 'stimulated importation of population' was likely to affect both halves of the county, and that the Society much regretted that overspill had not been considered jointly by both county councils. We know from the minutes that the SPS had first considered putting in a plea for a new town, but had decided that such a recommendation might be considered as lying outside the scope of the Society.

At the county council meeting, the Chairman of the Planning Committee stated that West Suffolk had to take a realistic view.

> The idea that West Suffolk could be left as an island undisturbed with a low density of population, while all around was subject to heavy pressure, was completely unrealistic. . . . Cosford RDC, he said, had asked for industrial development to provide suitable employment for the young people. . . . Side by side with that, the County was spending a substantial sum in fees on a report how best to preserve Lavenham.

The carefully detailed report by Donald Insall, *Lavenham past – present – future*, may have persuaded the West Suffolk County Council of the special importance of the town.

County Division of Overspill

Norman Scarfe, one of Suffolk's foremost historians, in a letter to the *East Anglian Daily Times* where the issue was hotly debated, pointed out that there were two overriding reasons why West Suffolk should not be used as a dumping ground

> for the people London doesn't want and is trying to unload onto the rest of the island. The first objection is that there appears to be no guarantee that those places in London will not immediately be filled by 40,000 immigrants from other parts of England, or from overseas. The second objection is that 40,000 is a large fraction – more than 30% – of the existing population of West Suffolk. In short even if the greatest care were taken, the whole society of West Suffolk people would undergo much the most revolutionary change in its history since the Norman Conquest, all in the interests of what appears to be an economic fallacy.

East Suffolk County Council's attitude to overspill was largely influenced by the early effects of the schemes for Haverhill and Bury St Edmunds, though initially the objections seemed to be strictly rational. There were 'no towns, capable of taking large-scale development, which are in an unsound economic condition'. Many did not agree with this verdict. Some Halesworth people, for instance, felt that its days as a market town were over and that they could do with two or three thousand extra people to infuse new blood into the town. Others felt that immigration, even on this scale, could bring supermarkets, which would kill local shops; large new factories, which would drive out smaller businesses; and that there would be enormous rises in rates.

The SPS, sticking to its constitutional aim of the protection of amenities, did not attempt as a body to enter into economic or political arguments, though some of its members did, in a private capacity. The Society held an open forum on 19 May 1961 on 'The Decentralization of London with Special Reference to Suffolk', at which Lord Euston, who had been the President for the last four years, took the Chair. The speakers were John Craig (for the LCC), the Vicar of Haverhill, James Gorst (County Planning Officer for West Suffolk) and C. S. Chettoe (for the CPRE).

The meeting seems to have done nothing to subdue the anxiety of the members of the SPS, even though the Haverhill experiment was pronounced a resounding success for the new population. (Not much was said about the feelings of the old inhabitants.) 'Bury St Edmunds,' said one speaker, 'had been one of the earliest of the "New Towns" when it had been founded in the eleventh century.' The members heard with increasing dismay that not only Bury St Edmunds, Sudbury and Hadleigh were to be vastly extended, but also that Lavenham and Clare, the two most precious of West Suffolk's small towns, were each to have 500 Londoners, as well as Elmswell, Glemsford and Stanton. So keen were West Suffolk County Council to take advantage of the arrangements, that they had actually increased the total asked of them by 4,500. Lord Euston, in his closing speech, suggested that, as many others felt, one new town might be better and do much less damage to Suffolk towns and countryside than so many individual smaller increases.

Mr Chettoe's report for the CPRE deplored this piecemeal system of the selection of towns for expansion and called for a national, or at least a regional, plan in which towns would be selected objectively according to their suitability, taking into account all relevant factors. 'If this were done,' he commented, 'it does not follow that Suffolk will be required to take the same number of people, area for area, as other counties, because the relevant factors would differ in each case.'

The main concern of the CPRE was the same as that of the SPS: the visual effect of the overspill proposals on the countryside and on the architecture in the towns. (The architecture, of course, interested the SPAB as well.)

Mr Chettoe did not consider the small towns in any way suitable for overspill; he thought Bury St Edmunds and Sudbury suitable only for reduced numbers (Sudbury and Great Cornard with a population of 8,500 were thought by the County Council to be capable of taking 7,000); but Mildenhall, Newmarket and Haverhill all seemed to him reasonable places to house the influx.

The South East Study 1961–81

The problems of the overspill movement had caused the Conservative Government of 1959–64 to set up the *South East Study 1961–81* under the Ministry of Housing and Local Government. The conclusions of this study were, among other things, that where existing towns were to be expanded, they must be large and have a good economic potential for expansion. They should not be less than seventy miles from London, so that there would be no merging, and it should be expected that the population would be increased by 50 to 100 per cent.

The Expansion of Ipswich

By 1965, the Minister for the new Labour Government, Richard Crossman, had confirmed Peterborough, Northampton and Ipswich as suitable towns in the

THE GROWTH OF DEVELOPMENT IN IPSWICH

1920

1920—1951

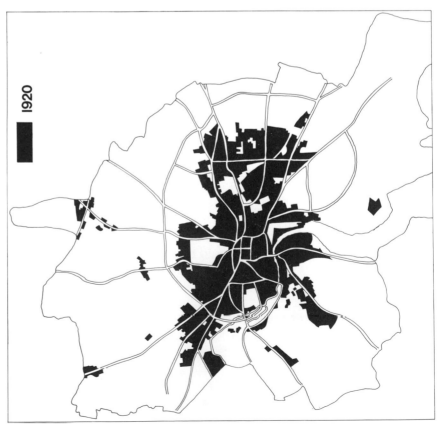

1920

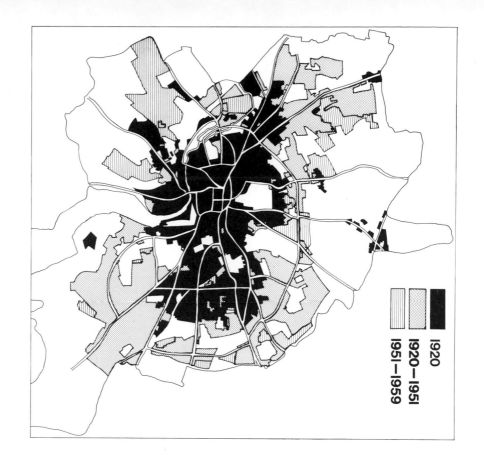

1920

1920—1951

1951—1959

1920

1920—1951

1951—1959

1959—1972

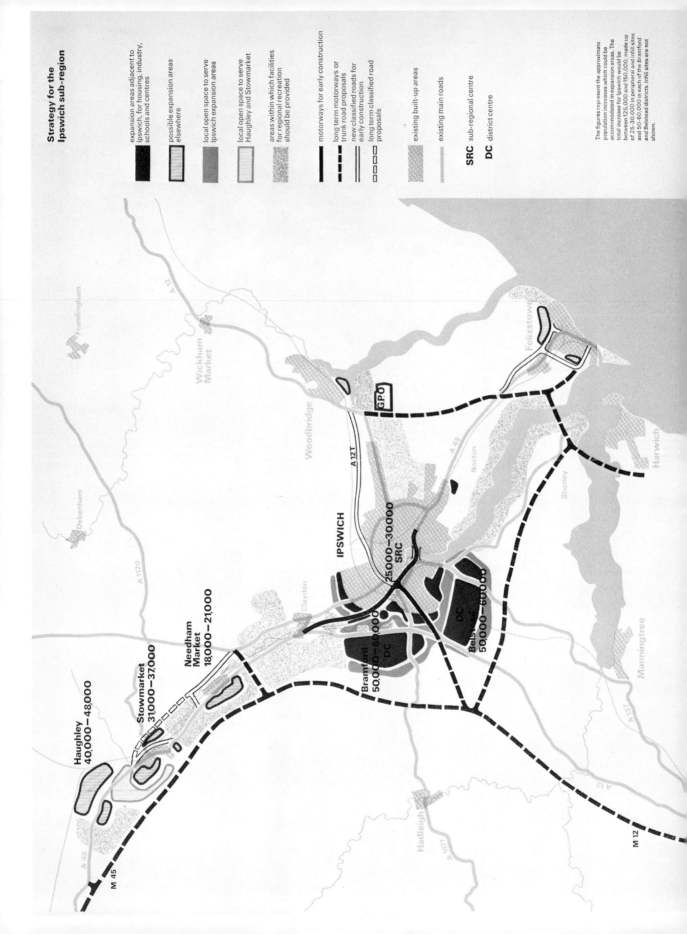

Strategy for the Ipswich sub-region

expansion areas adjacent to Ipswich, for housing, industry, schools and centres

possible expansion areas elsewhere

local open space to serve Ipswich expansion areas

local open space to serve Haughley and Stowmarket

areas within which facilities for regional recreation should be provided

motorways for early construction

long term motorways or trunk road proposals

new classified roads for early construction

long term classified road proposals

existing built-up areas

existing main roads

SRC   sub-regional centre

DC   district centre

The figures represent the approximate population increases which could be accommodated in expansion areas. The total increase for Ipswich would be between 125,000 and 150,000, made up of 25-30,000 in peripheral and infill sites and 50-60,000 in each of the Bramford and Belstead districts. Infill sites are not shown.

Framlingham

Wickham Market

Woodbridge

Felixstowe

GPO

A12T

A45

Nacton

Shotley

Harwich

Debenham

A1120

IPSWICH

25,000–30,000
SRC

Claydon

Bramford
50,000–60,000
DC

Belstead
50,000–60,000
DC

Manningtree

A137

Needham Market
18,000–21,000

Stowmarket
31,000–37,000

Haughley
40,000–48,000

Hadleigh

A1071

A12

M 12

A 45

M 45

A dormitory village for Ipswich: Capel St Mary. Uninspired design enlivened by residents' own efforts in their gardens.

Eastern Counties, and preparations were going ahead to plan for their growth. For Ipswich, Shankland, Cox & Associates were selected to produce proposals. In 1966, they published the result of their study of the implications of absorbing 70,000 Londoners into Ipswich and the surrounding area by 1981. The report, *The Expansion of Ipswich*, caused something of a sensation, not only for the people of Ipswich but for those in the designated area, for the consultants' brief included planning for an even longer-term strategy reaching to the turn of the century. A town like Needham Market might possibly see a staggering population increase from 1,700 to 21,000.

For the SPS, this prospect of planned growth presented a new kind of challenge. The basic proposals, unlike those of the overspill programme, could not be argued with, and in a few months this scheme (with a certain population increase for Ipswich of 50 per cent) had to be absorbed and commented on in a practical and positive way. It was a far cry from the small individual cases of earlier days, but, by good fortune, the Society had in its Chairman, Sir Joshua Rowley, and in Norman Scarfe, people with experience and skill in responding constructively. The Ipswich Society, formed in 1960 with an enlightened chairman and committee dedicated to the protection of the diminished medieval and considerable Victorian

The plan that went wrong. Ipswich people were not to be led away from their traditional shopping streets. Greyfriars won a television award for the ugliest building in East Anglia.

heritage of the town, joined forces with the SPS to keep in close contact with the planners and give them all the help they could. If Ipswich, they felt, *had* to become a new town, the transformation must be as successful as possible.

It could be argued, even today, that Shankland, Cox's carefully structured scheme might have solved many of the problems which conservationists now face. An overall planning policy might have resulted, in spite of the enormous intake of population, in a much better balance between town and country, much less haphazard and unsuitable development, and a more satisfactory solution of traffic problems than the present piecemeal arrangements. This, at any rate, was the thinking at that time of many members of the SPS, who realized that, with such a government-sponsored scheme, there would have been enough money to spend on improving the centre of Ipswich and providing facilities for education and recreation which would otherwise be unobtainable. Other members feared the possible swamping of the smaller towns included in the sub-region once the initial areas, Belstead and Bramford, had been filled. The Needham Market Society started in 1966, not as a protest group, but as a body which felt that these

A building that stirs the emotions – of love or hate. Willis, Faber & Dumas' Ipswich head-quarters, thought by some to be the most distinguished modern building in Suffolk; by others to be out of sympathy in scale and materials with everything that surrounds it.

towns themselves should be given a voice in their future. There was also consider-able emotional feeling against a loss of identity by being more closely linked with London. Ipswich, although the closest to London of all the sub-regions, was the nearest town, as the report pointed out, with its own daily morning paper, and it retained a strong character of independence. Suffolk had in fact for many years been the county where London influence stopped and a real regional identity began. This was not to be given up lightly.

A change of government, however, put an end to the vast schemes that the south-eastern study had set in motion. The Shankland, Cox plan was abandoned.

Woodbridge Tide Mill before its rescue and restoration. In 1968 the rapidly decaying building was purchased by Mrs R. T. Gardner. With the aid of local people and substantial grants, it is now preserved and open to the public.

7 Battles

While successive governments had been energetically reorganizing the country's population, they were also responding to public pressure for greater care in the preservation of what was left of the English countryside and the architectural heritage.

With the coming of peace, Hugh Dalton, as Chancellor of the Exchequer in the Labour Government which came to power in July 1945, introduced the National Land Fund: £50 million to be spent on the upkeep of historic buildings and the saving of works of art, as a national thanksgiving. By 1950, so many great country houses had been lost that Sir Ernest Gowers was asked to form a committee to inquire into the situation, suggest possible solutions and report back to Parliament. Three years later, a Bill was passed by Parliament implementing many of the proposals, and the Historic Buildings Council, empowered to give grants for the preservation of listed buildings, was set up. The Land Fund money was not spent. It stayed gathering dust and interest. After thirty-three years, it now seems that the present Government's proposed Heritage Fund may resolve the controversies which have arisen over its use.

In the years following the war, in spite of the rise of the local amenity society, there was still widespread apathy about conservation. It was among the older and better off that the greatest interest in architecture and the landscape appeared. It was hard, though the planners and consultants were not to blame, to get any response to the expensively produced copies of town plans and surveys, except from those who had always taken an interest in such things. Even when proposals which would radically alter their lives were presented to the inhabitants of towns and villages, they seemed unable, until it was too late, to voice any kind of opinion. When, in 1964, there were plans to build over the fields of East Bergholt, a proposal which would have doubled the population as well as completely altering the historic shape of the village, it was, as usual, mainly the non-natives who foresaw what these changes might mean, not only to their own village but to the whole character of Constable Country. At that date, with a fairly loose strategy of planning in East Suffolk, it was still possible for a landowner to attempt to initiate a massive change in size of the built-up area of a village.

The Survey of Dedham Vale

But good docs sometimes come out of bad. The possible expansion of East Bergholt and proposals for large-scale development at Stratford St Mary and the hotly contested public inquiry that it generated (the SPS was strongly represented in spite of its Regional Correspondent saying that the inquiry was certain to be lost) resulted in the Ministry's decision against the most objectionable features of the plan; and, at the direction of the Minister, Essex County Council, together with

Needham Market Station before and after removal of the canopies. The canopy has recently been replaced by British Rail after enforcement action was taken by Mid Suffolk District Council.

The SPS has been fighting for the saving of Newmarket Old Station for more than a decade.

Ashman's Hall, Barsham, built circa 1817. The SPS has been pressing for many years for its restoration.

the county councils of East and West Suffolk, produced their *Survey of Dedham Vale* in 1966.

The *Survey of Dedham Vale*, prepared at the suggestion of the Minister of Housing and Local Government, was an important milestone in the history of planning in Suffolk. Its conclusions, and the recommendations that stemmed from it two years later, were directed at 'redressing any existing harmful features which detract from the character of the Vale'. Unfortunately, the harmful features, or most of them, were already a year or two old, and short of pulling down large numbers of new houses, uprooting kerbstones and unmaking access roads, there was no way of curing the new suburbanization of Stratford St Mary and East Bergholt.

Eastgate Bridge, Bury St Edmunds. Plans to rebuild it and replace the iron railings were fought by the SPS.

Rural Settlement Policy

By the time the survey was published, East Suffolk County Council had strengthened its rural settlement policy. Towns and villages were classified for settlement purposes into graded categories which set out the scale of development considered to be appropriate for each one, so that, what with intensive pressure from outside the county from people wishing to settle there, it was inevitable that the face of Suffolk should begin to change in some places almost out of recognition. The settlement policy was designed to direct development so as to enable a more efficient arrangement to be made of the whole range of public services. But in spite of the declared aim that any development should have regard to preserving

Detail from View of Dedham *by John Constable, 1814. This famous panorama is surprisingly more heavily wooded today. However, the* Dedham Vale Landscape Study, *carried out by Essex and Suffolk County Councils, shows that there is a disturbing amount of mature and post-mature vegetation which threatens the future quality of the landscape. The introduction of a different type of drainage scheme could also bring about drastic changes.*

the character of existing villages and countryside, it is sad to recall that, in effect, more harm was done to the countryside at this time, and more quickly, than perhaps at any other.

How often were residents assured that buildings put up would be 'well designed', and then disappointed to find that they turned out to be merely expensive and pretentious? Glib assurances were offered that new developments would be 'landscaped', as if it were possible to create in six months what it had taken a thousand years to evolve. Anxious neighbours would see two smartly dressed young men measuring up a likely looking road frontage and know that in a short time a dozen houses with pocket-handkerchief gardens, built of the same materials and to the same designs as others being erected in Cornwall or Yorkshire, would spring up like mushrooms. Nor was it only outsiders who were responsible for the suburbanization of the villages. There were plenty of farmers and landowners ready to sell at the much inflated prices being paid for land with planning permission. The local councils' office tables must have been piled with applications from owners of land in development zones.

Of course, additions to the population, where they came gradually and not in overwhelming numbers, brought good things too. Newcomers often took a

Sudbury Town Hall.

greater interest than established residents in the history of the villages, formed groups and societies, and were quick to involve themselves in local affairs. Most of Suffolk's fifteen amenity societies were founded in the 1960s or early 1970s, often by people who had lived in her towns or villages for only a few years.

Sudbury and Bury St Edmunds

This was a decade of constant problems for the SPS, and for anyone concerned to keep Suffolk as one of the few essentially rural counties left in England. Those that cared for Suffolk were often accused, by those who were busily exploiting the countryside for their own ends, of being backward-looking or of being selfish, as if it were morally excusable to ruin yet more of England because much of it was ruined already. Certain people who wished a building out of the way were all too ready to label it 'old-fashioned', 'a white elephant', 'an eyesore', or 'a derelict monstrosity'. Their prime targets were often Georgian and Victorian buildings. Speculative eyes were cast on Gainsborough's house in Sudbury, and then on the Town Hall, built in 1833, and still one of the ornaments of Sudbury's Market Hill.

A few years later it was the Corn Exchange which came under attack, and the whole of Market Hill was threatened with redevelopment. Poor Sudbury, having had its outskirts disfigured by industrial and residential estates of the meanest design, only retained its important buildings by the efforts of a few who managed to persuade the authorities to change their minds. West Suffolk County Council,

Sudbury Corn Exchange: once threatened with demolition, it is now the town's library.

Rebuilding in Bury St Edmunds Conservation Area. The SPS and the Bury Society succeeded in getting a better-designed scheme including the re-use of the eighteenth-century doorcase and nineteenth-century shop front.

responding to growing public pressure, produced and carried out the successful conversion of the Corn Exchange to a Public Library in 1964.

Sixteen miles away, at almost the same time, at Bury St Edmunds, that jewel of West Suffolk, the Borough Council were eagerly preparing a scheme for the redevelopment of the Cornhill and the neighbouring area, dismissing the two listed buildings which they proposed to tear down, the Corn Exchange and the Public Library, as, in the first case, 'somewhat dull and uninteresting', and as, in

The Theatre Royal, Bury St Edmunds, restored to active life by enthusiasts.

the second, more cautiously, 'appearing' to be of 'no great architectural merit' – as though architectural merit could be hidden.

The Earl of Euston (later Duke of Grafton), the President of the SPS and one of the leading figures in the international field of conservation, led the Society into battle alongside the Georgian Group, the Victorian Society and a host of private objectors from Bury St Edmunds itself and other places in Suffolk. For once, opposition came from all parts of the community: the farmers, who mistrusted the moving of their centre of trade to a new site; the shopkeepers, who feared the influx of chainstores; the ratepayers, who could see nothing in the scheme but a sharp increase in their rates; and the ordinary people of Bury, who loved their town and its harmonious mixture of buildings. The objectors were unimpressed by assurances that one of the designs for the new shopping centre and its 'multi-purpose' Corn Exchange had been drawn up by the architect for the new Canterbury development. Canterbury had been bombed and needed new buildings. Bury St Edmunds had not.

Such massive opposition ensured the defeat of the central development scheme

A cause of dissent among SPS members. In 1966 the Ministry of Works proposed to unpick the eighteenth- and nineteenth-century houses from the ruins of Bury St Edmunds Abbey. A majority of the Executive Committee was in favour of retaining the houses. The Suffolk Building Preservation Trust is currently (1980) discussing the restoration of No. 3 with the Borough.

and West Suffolk County Council initiated the restoration of the Cornhill area with a conversion of the Corn Exchange, though even here the SPS and the Victorian Society had to press for a better design than the one first proposed. By 1970, the Robert Adam Town Hall had been developed as an Exhibition Centre, partly financed by an appeal to the local community, and the future of most of the public buildings of Bury was made tolerably safe.

Fortunately for Bury, there were plenty of people in West Suffolk who were sufficiently interested in its historic buildings to want to revive them for the use of the town. Some of these, while the arguments raged about the Cornhill, were planning to restore the Theatre Royal, designed in 1819 by William Wilkins, the architect of the National Gallery and St George's Hospital in London, and return it to its proper function. The theatre had been used by Greene King Ltd, the local brewers, as a store for the past thirty-five years, and it was through their gener-

Plans for a monstrous redevelopment of Bury St Edmunds Cornhill which would have dwarfed the Robert Adam Town Hall were mercifully scrapped after a protracted battle in 1960. Later the SPS successfully prevented an inappropriate conversion of the Town Hall.

92

The Barnaby Almshouses of 1826 in College Street, Bury St Edmunds. These white-brick buildings will be converted back to dwellings.

osity that the building became available. The Borough Council, having given consideration to the project, decided on the grounds of cost, the dangerous nature of the corner on which the building was situated, and its remoteness from convenient car parks (the nearest car park must have been all of five minutes walk away), not to support the scheme. Nothing daunted, the action group carried on, receiving support from the Historic Buildings Council and many local firms and organizations. The result was a fine example of what determination, hard work, persuasiveness and idealism can do. The theatre was successfully restored to its original function.

The Great Churchyard, Bury St Edmunds. Graveyards are often the only places surviving in towns where wildlife can flourish. A 1968 scheme to 'landscape' the site would have introduced a jarring note. Today a simple management scheme ensures its continued informality.

Moreton Hall

All this activity was taking place in the decade between 1960 and 1970 against the background of the overspill problem and the possible arrival of 10,000 or even 20,000 newcomers. The reality caused far less upheaval than was expected; by 1976, only just over 4,000 migrants had settled in Bury. The SPS, though, was much exercised about the effect of the promised new industrial sites, as well as the residential ones which the new population would need. The Bury St Edmunds

94

town map of 1962 included in its proposed building sites one of the areas which made a vital contribution to the character of the town: the glimpse from Abbeygate Street, over the Abbey ruins, of open country round Moreton Hall. This, in the Society's opinion, was one of the rare charms of a town of such a size; one of the few places where the feeling of a medieval town, with its sharply defined edge, could really be caught. The Committee were alarmed by the tendency which was emerging at Bury of building upwards (a block of twelve storeys was already under construction in the town), and pressed the Ministry of Housing and Local Government to impose limitations on the height of a new building – not more than three storeys – on the land overlooking the Abbey Gardens; and, with the support of the Royal Fine Arts Commission, that was agreed by the County Council.

The Moreton Hall issue continued to worry the SPS for several years. At the Bury St Edmunds Town Map Public Inquiry, in July 1963, the Society's written objections were joined by others, even more forcefully worded, from the SPAB and CPRE. In reply, West Suffolk planners stressed the need for recouping the cost of road widening necessary to feed the industrial area by developing the Moreton Hall site.

> The opposition's main argument that the town would be denied the green back-drop of Moreton Hall [they said] was invalid as it was scarcely visible at ground level from anywhere in the town.

Another inquiry into proposed revisions of the town map, in 1968, gave the Society a fresh opportunity to stress the importance of the need to keep the view open, but, on the publication of the plan, the Committee were distressed to find that the town map, approved by the Department of the Environment which had been formed since the Public Inquiry, included the whole of the Moreton Hall site. Together with the newly formed Bury St Edmunds Society, they put up a strong representation against the loss of such a precious feature of the town, engaging a landscape architect to produce a report which would clarify their position with both local and national authorities. With support again from the Royal Fine Arts Commission, a compromise was reached and the view was partially saved. Without the intervention of the two societies, the unique combination of a town and field would have been lost.

New Professionalism

The quickening of the pace of changes that took place during the early 1960s put far more pressure on the SPS Committee than ever before. Its make-up had changed somewhat from that of earlier days; there were fewer scholars and clergymen, more farmers and landowners, a sprinkling of architects and a good attendance of representatives from the two county councils. These people found themselves obliged in a very short space of time to pick their way through a maze of new regulations, to learn to cope with the profusion of town maps and surveys and to try to accommodate, within their expressions of opinion, an understanding of the new problems that faced the planners, as well as their first object: the

Lavenham before and after the removal of overhead electricity lines by the Eastern Electricity Board.

preservation of the essential character of Suffolk. Under the chairmanship of Francis Engleheart, there had still been a charming element of amateurishness which may have made some local authorities a trifle impatient. All voluntary societies have to beware of the cry of, 'Oh, it's *them* complaining again!' and, undoubtedly, Sir Joshua Rowley, who became Chairman on Mr Engleheart's death, was, as a member of the County Council, well aware of the attitude that his colleagues might take to the Society's observations. His intention to get the SPS taken seriously, as a positive influence, was quickly responded to by some of his Committee. In March 1965, the Executive Committee was presented with a short but thoughtful paper by Jean Corke urging the Society to take up the suggestion of the Civic Trust and the CPRE that amenity societies should make pictorial surveys of towns to assist planning committees, something much more than an illustrated list of buildings.

An assessment of the special areas, the relative importance of individual buildings or groups of buildings on the whole, the sequence of spaces which buildings define between them (spaces being often just as much a heritage as bricks
and mortar), streets with particularly good effects of closure, say a church spire
or a good skyline or a distant view of the countryside beyond.

She pointed out that models were not enough on their own; the pictorial survey
would give 'literally the view of the man in the street'.

Such ideas are now taken for granted by those familiar with the surveys of the
last ten years, but, for the SPS, and indeed for the planners, here was something
new. One or two members were a little nervous of such an innovation, it would be
a massive task, care must be taken not to give the impression that the Society was
the sole arbiter of taste in the county, and so on. East Suffolk planners, at least,

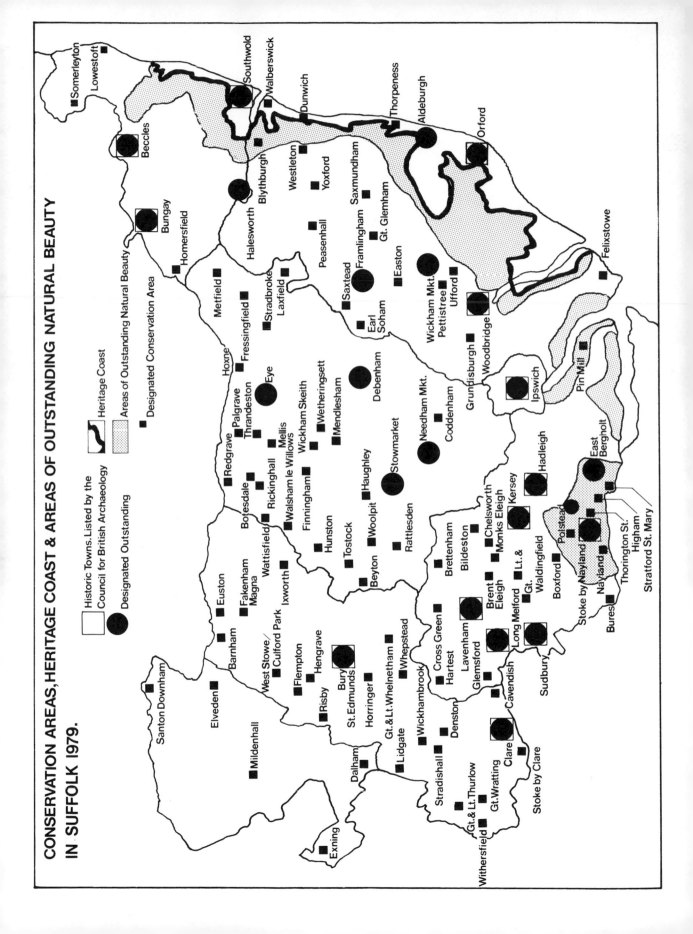

CONSERVATION AREAS, HERITAGE COAST & AREAS OF OUTSTANDING NATURAL BEAUTY IN SUFFOLK 1979.

Historic Towns. Listed by the Council for British Archaeology

Designated Outstanding

Heritage Coast

Areas of Outstanding Natural Beauty

Designated Conservation Area

Industry in the countryside.

seem to have had no such reservations. Besides being ready to listen to SPS views on the surveys already in hand for Beccles and Woodbridge, the County Planning Officer undertook to provide the sub-committee set up to deal with the surveys with a scheme of guidance which would make co-operation easier. By the following year, the SPS had, with its own team of surveyors led by Norman Scarfe and Mrs Corke, drawn up its own reports on Woodbridge, Eye and Bungay. For the next five years, East Suffolk used the reports of this team as the basis for the sections on the visual aspects of nearly all the town surveys.

The enthusiasm of the Town Studies Sub-committee, apart from contributing in an expert way to the actual understanding of the towns themselves, spread to the

Car breaker's dump.

organizing of an exhibition and a pamphlet written by Jean Corke, *Growth and Change in the Suffolk Village*, which expounded the ideas on which the studies had been carried out. Here, at least, the Society was beginning, as the former Chairman had hoped, to be taken seriously. It was now participating in the planning of the county, rather than simply commenting on proposals.

Eastern Federation of Amenity Societies

During this period there had been much talk of forming an association of all the amenity societies in the eastern counties. In 1966, the Eastern Federation of

Car breaker's yard: a happier solution.

Amenity Societies (EFAS) was formed. Its objects were to promote and encourage high standards of architecture and town and country planning, and to stimulate public interest in all aspects of amenity work.

EFAS held one of its earliest conferences in Hadleigh, and under the direction of Elizabeth Chesterton, the distinguished town planning expert, carried out a town study which was of assistance to the planners in giving that rather underrated town a new importance in the eyes of Suffolk dwellers. (Only a year or two before, it had been criticized, by someone who wanted to develop its western side, as being unbalanced, a 'fault' which could only have been noticed from an aeroplane!)

Wissington Church and Barns.

Conservation Areas

But, to many people in the Society, there was no perceptible change in the influence that was brought to bear on the outside world. Though the large expansion schemes had, on the whole, either been accomplished or abandoned, there were still constant and disturbing changes which ate away at the essential Suffolk and did almost as much harm. The creation of Conservation Areas did have some effect in stabilizing the important parts of towns and villages. In 1967, Duncan Sandys, the chairman of the Civic Trust, had introduced a Private Members Bill which came into force as the Civic Amenities Act. This empowered local authorities to designate Conservation Areas by picking out those areas which

Lack of protection for farm buildings can result in destruction of an irreplaceable group: Wissington spoilt by insensitive new building.

were of special character worthy of being *conserved*; that is, not simply protected but positively enhanced. Where there were to be changes, they were to be sympathetically handled, but the Act itself gave no special powers to local authorities beyond a requirement to advertise any proposals for development. East and West Suffolk, as in so many other cases, took quite different attitudes to the new idea. In the east, parts of Beccles, Woodbridge and East Bergholt were designated at first, and thirty-nine other areas proposed. The preference here was for small, compact areas. As late as 1972, only three areas of West Suffolk had been desig-

Signpost madness in the centre of Newmarket.

nated, though they were much larger and more loosely defined. The new designations were not always greeted with great enthusiasm; while some people felt flattered by being thought to live in a place of visual importance, others were irked by the restrictions on alteration or development of their properties. Some conservationists worried that tight controls in these areas would result in over-development of less fortunate places – a worry that had some foundation in a few towns and villages.

The Countryside, Agriculture and Suburbanization

While the historic towns were beginning to be more appreciated, there was a good deal of anger at the damage caused to natural features. Trees were felled, hedges grubbed out or scorched by careless stubble-burning, and the air was often heavy, not with the scent of hay or good, honest manure, but with unidentifiable chemical smells. The country, many people felt, was being attacked by farmers intent on increased production at the expense of other values. This, though deplorable in visual terms, was at least understandable. But here was the tangible evidence of what had been foreseen so many years ago: the recurrent conflict between conservation and agriculture. Official attitudes were hardly helpful to the layman's understanding of the problem: on the one hand, legislation for the enhancement of the landscape; and on the other, government grants for improvement in food production, and, for a time, even for the bulldozing of hedges.

Smaller changes produced equally strong reactions. The SPS and the newspapers received a continual stream of letters about the urbanization of the countryside: village greens and even quite tiny triangles of grass being surrounded by kerbstones, bridges being reconstructed with unpleasant mesh sides, fords and streams disappearing into culverts. Even the wild flowers, which gave so much innocent pleasure on the roadside verges, vanished with over-enthusiastic cutting. These changes, and above all those concerning trees, made many people, and not only the SPS members, extremely angry. It has taken not only the botanist but also the historian to begin a revival of sensible management which will ensure that at least some of our ancient woodland survives.

Felsham Hall and Monks Park Woods

In 1968, two such experts played a major part in a public inquiry, which was the first important fight to save part of Suffolk's landscape. Felsham Hall Wood and Monks Park Wood near Bury St Edmunds, probably the largest remaining area of ancient woodland in Suffolk, became a matter of public concern to the people of Bradfield St George. A large part of Monks Park Wood had been cleared for arable farming, but local residents managed to obtain an Emergency Tree Preservation Order on the remainder. West Suffolk County Council, while sympathetic to the pleas for saving the woods on the grounds of their ecological and historic interest, were only able to insist on a fringe of trees being kept, as their powers extended only to 'the visual and aesthetic aspects of rural conservation'. A ludicrous situation: on the one side, the Ministry of Agriculture promising a grant for reclaiming the land; on the other, the Ministry of Housing and Local Government being asked to confirm a Tree Preservation Order!

Though the many people who knew and loved the woods could, on their own, have made an impressive case for their preservation, the day was won by the expert knowledge of David Dymond, himself a local resident and the Resident Tutor in Suffolk of the Cambridge Board of Extra-Mural Studies, coupled with that of Oliver Rackham, then University Demonstrator in Botany at Cambridge. Between them they ensured that the woodland, clearly identified as belonging to Bury St Edmunds Abbey in 1121 and coppiced by the thirteenth century at the

Farm buildings have little protection except when listed. Even that safeguard failed to keep this magnificent Wherstead barn on site. It was removed to another county for conversion into a house.

latest, could be saved and handed over to the Society for the Promotion of Nature Reserves as an object-lesson in history, ecology and also in preservation.

The SPS, while leaving the case in the hands of Mr Dymond, nevertheless felt the importance of such a victory. The new Secretary, E. Field Reid, who had initiated the production of a much-needed newsletter to keep members informed of the Society's activities, summed up the growing consciousness of the importance of landscape:

The episode, and its aftermath, have emphasized the need for the most active vigilance by the Society, who often find themselves thinking exclusively in terms of preserving bricks and mortar, and forgetting the business of seeing the landscape *whole*.

While the argument over the Bradfield woods was in progress, another large and important part of Suffolk's landscape, which had hitherto been rather ignored both by the Council Council and the SPS, was being reappraised.

Areas of Outstanding Natural Beauty and Heritage Coast

Under the National Park and Access to the Countryside Act 1949, the National Parks Commission was formed and entrusted with the designation not only of National Parks but also with Areas of Outstanding Natural Beauty (AONBs). The Countryside Commission, instituted as the result of a further Act in 1968, took over as the designating body, and local planning authorities were given powers to preserve and enhance the areas and to obtain Exchequer grants for this purpose. Under the National Parks Commission, only part of Dedham Vale had been designated in Suffolk, and now the coastal area came under the scrutiny of the planning authorities.

The East Suffolk Planning Officer produced a report, *Suffolk Coasts and Heaths, Proposed Areas of Outstanding Natural Beauty*, which suggested a band of protected land stretching from Kessingland to the mouth of the Deben, and joining, on the north bank of the Stour, the AONB already existing in Dedham Vale. The SPS pressed for the inclusion of the whole of the Deben and Orwell estuaries, which made an almost unbroken line from Lowestoft to Shotley.

In 1970, the Minister of Housing and Local Government confirmed the area, which included all that the SPS had pressed for, by the new title of Heritage Coast. It was one of forty such areas in England and Wales. Four years later, a Heritage Coast Officer was appointed to promote the conservation of the area's natural character.

Snake's head fritillary at Framsden, where the meadow is open to the public on two days in the year.

8 The 1970s

Professional Inhabitants

The 1960s had stretched the talents and resources of energy of the SPS infinitely further than they had ever been stretched before. The Society contained people of the highest calibre, some well known in Suffolk, others working quietly behind the scenes – architects, historians, landowners, housewives – all giving time and thought to the business of adapting Suffolk to its new way of life without betraying its character. But they all knew that they had very little power without a large body of support behind them. Norman Scarfe, at the Public Inquiry on the Shankland, Cox plan for Ipswich, had sounded a note of warning:

> . . . the problems of preserving the character of the familiar *environment*, to ensure a proper continuity between past, present and future, are so many of them of a kind that have been given virtually no *professional* study. There are professional economists, planners, agriculturalists, but there are no *professional inhabitants*, no professional students of this particular human environment. But this does not exonerate any of us from the duty to the existing inhabitants of Suffolk to try to preserve at the very least, the best things in the world that they are used to and feel at home in.

These were stirring words to usher in the 1970s and the fifth decade of the Society's life. Mrs Schofield would have approved of the expression 'professional inhabitants', a logical extension of her own aim of education and of changing the 'climate of opinion'. The Society began to turn its attention to publications. In 1970, the two county councils asked the SPS to undertake two independent town studies, one of Stowmarket and the other, a larger task, of Bury St Edmunds. Both investigating teams consisted of a number of professionals; the Bury surveyors included, as well as David Dymond and Norman Scarfe, Jack Penton, a designer with long experience of vernacular architecture, J. B. Weller, a knowledgeable architect, and Sylvia Colman, one of Suffolk's experts on timber-framed buildings. The 2,000 copies that were printed for the SPS were sold not only among the 1,000-strong membership, but to other organizations in England, and as far away as Switzerland and Australia.

Publications

In 1972 came another publication, one which helped to bring into being a new and important body. The Rev. (now Canon) John Fitch, Rector of Brandon, distressed by the growing number of redundancies among Suffolk's 500-odd medieval churches, was moved to make a detailed survey of the problems of saving them from disuse and decay. Though the SPS had, on the whole, been involved with

Woodbridge church porch: mid fifteenth-century flint and stone flush work.

churches only in a limited way up till now, usually leaving the bulk of cases to the Redundant Churches Fund or the Friends of Friendless Churches, the quality of Mr Fitch's memorandum made it imperative to spread its message as far as possible. The difficulty was to spread it far enough. It should have been obligatory reading for any minister of any denomination, combining as it did a high degree of sensitivity with solid facts and inescapable common sense. Not only was it an admirable piece of writing, but the presentation of the book, with illustrations by Christina Newns, who worked regularly for the SPS, lived up to the maxim of the Secretary, E. Field Reid: 'A society that sets high standards for visual factors in the environment must produce a high standard in design.'

The newsletter, in its new format, was another example of this way of thinking. The Secretary had never been afraid to devote almost a whole issue to a topic of great importance. In 1970, he had included a fascinating and provocative talk, 'Farming: Planning: Conservation', by J. B. Weller, because the attendance at the AGM at which it had been given had been so small. The following year he included the evidence given by the representatives of the SPS at the public inquiry on Tattingstone Reservoir.

But the organization of the Society, in spite of the newsletter, still did not involve more than a small number of active members. The Regional Correspondents were not all conscientious, and though the Council still met, it did not fulfil a very useful function. There was perhaps more than ever a distinction between the Executive and the general membership, who, through no fault of their own, remained passive. But new developments were at hand which were to give the members more opportunity of participating in the work of the Society.

Suffolk Building Preservation Trust

The first few years of the 1970s were remarkable for the number of new measures, both local and national, that affected the SPS. In 1971, a legacy of £7,800 was the starting point for something which had been thought of forty years earlier: the Suffolk Building Preservation Trust. Ever since Hilda Mason had put the proposal forward, so long ago, the idea of a 'Cottage Improvement Trust' had been discussed and planned for by successive committees. Now, with the encouragement of the Duke of Grafton, the Chairman, Henry Engleheart (son of the former Chairman), was able to announce its inception. The benefactor, Mr F. H. Bowcher of Higham, was described by Mr Engleheart as having been a friend of Sir Alfred Munnings.

> They were great friends and very much twin souls with a great love of horses and the Suffolk countryside. I only met him once and I chiefly remember an extremely old and battered car outside the house; and inside, Mr Bowcher vigorously shovelling sugar into his claret which had to be of good quality to meet with his approval!

The first acquisition of the Trust was a pair of fine seventeenth-century houses at Rickinghall. As listed buildings, they became the subject of an inquiry when it was proposed to demolish them. The fact that the Trust was prepared to restore them undoubtedly influenced the inspector at the inquiry to refuse permission for demolition.

Beccles Bell Tower, restored by the townspeople.

Suffolk Historic Churches Trust

Shortly after the formation of the Building Trust, the Duke of Grafton proposed another new venture, first thought of as 'The Friends of Suffolk Churches' but, by 1973, registered as 'The Suffolk Historic Churches Trust'. Though initiated and manned almost entirely by SPS members, and founded with a donation from SPS funds, the Trust retains a completely separate existence.

This year was one of such excitement for the Society's administrators that it is quite surprising to find how effectively they managed to deal with their casework, for it was in February 1973 that the Executive was told of a rare piece of good fortune. In 1944, the Gayer-Anderson brothers had presented Surrey County Council with the freehold of Little Hall and two small cottages in the Market Place at Lavenham for the use of art students, apparently because their friend Reginald Brill was principal of the Kingston College of Art. By 1973, some years after the brothers' death, the 'Gayer-Anderson Hostel for Art Students' was no longer a viable concern, and, after offering the buildings to the National Trust and West Suffolk County Council without success, the trustees turned to the Suffolk Building Preservation Trust, proposing to hand over not only the houses but also the considerable collection of books, pictures and furniture which was still housed in Little Hall, as well as a small endowment. Here, it seemed, was the ideal site for the headquarters which the SPS had wanted for many years; and it could hardly have found a more appropriate building.

Director

Having got the headquarters, the Society was not quite sure whom to install in it. As if by magic, the next piece of good fortune followed. An anonymous benefactor made an offer of a large annual sum so that a professional Field Officer could be appointed to enable the Society to handle its increasingly complicated affairs with expertise and to make it possible to initiate schemes which would increase the Society's influence in the county. In a remarkably short space of time, candidates had been interviewed and the Trust Fund set up, so that, by January 1974, the Field Director, as he was now called, was chosen out of a number of extremely well-qualified candidates.

The new Director was John Popham, a chartered surveyor who had specialized in conservation. He immediately set about reviewing the administration of the Society and its constitution, and had, at the end of six months, produced a comprehensive report covering all aspects of the future conduct of the Society.

He saw his appointment as an opportunity for the Society to begin to influence county policy before, rather than after, it had been formed. He saw a need for more frequent communication with the members, by means of a regular quarterly newsletter, and for a much more vigorous educational policy, and suggested the formation of sub-committees to deal with finance, membership, publicity, education and so on. He also wanted to see the Council disbanded; its membership was now ninety-strong, but its twice-yearly meetings were poorly attended and the cost of sending out minutes and other important papers was disproportionate to the benefit obtained. The Executive should be the managing body and should consist of not more than twenty-four members, including the officers, who now

Laxfield Church: one of over two hundred churches that have received grants from the Suffolk Historic Churches Trust.

numbered five, including a Membership Secretary, since the volume of work for the Hon. Secretary had increased so much.

Local Government Reorganization

The Director's report emphasized the importance of the newly formed SPS district committees, drawn from SPS members within each of the new local government district boundaries, resulting from local government reorganization in 1974. Each of the six local government districts now had its own planning officer with a much larger staff than those which had assisted the sometimes unqualified officers of the old rural district councils. In spite of the realization that these and other services provided by the new district councils would inevitably mean increases in the rates, most people with an interest in conservation were hopeful that a more expert staffing would bring about improvement in general planning and in co-operation between amenity societies and planners. There was now one county council for the whole of Suffolk, which retained control of planning strategy, but, in obedience to the requirements of central government, handed over detailed planning powers to the districts.

Conservationists were not so happy about other reorganization proposals, particularly those which involved county boundary changes. A government circular recommended gaining a small piece of Cambridgeshire and a sizeable chunk of Essex, taking in Colchester and extending to the Blackwater estuary, and losing a triangle of Suffolk from Southwold to Yarmouth. These ideas were greeted with alarm by many of those living in the areas, and were disturbing to anyone with a sense of history.

> Happily [in Norman Scarfe's words] the White Paper of 4 November 1971 announced second thoughts and, so far as Suffolk was concerned, abandoned the idea of scrapping, over wide areas of the two counties (East and West Suffolk), nine centuries of territorial allegiance.

There was, however, a small change in the north of the county which meant, in the regrettable loss of five parishes, that St Olaves wind pump, which had received the SPS's money and attention for many years, was transferred to Norfolk.

SPS District Committees

The SPS's own district committees consisted of ten or twelve members, each with a number of parishes under his care – a much more manageable area than the Regional Correspondents had dealt with. One or two of their number inspected the planning registers each week and distributed plans of anything likely to concern the SPS to the appropriate people. In this way, it was possible to keep a keen eye on all new developments, large or small, including applications involving listed buildings; and a general view of what was happening to the visual side of Suffolk could be easily kept in perspective. On the whole, the idea of these committees worked, and is still working well. Of course there are difficulties, not least of which is finding people with a reasonable understanding of architecture and enough imagination to see in their mind's eye the product of an architect's drawing and plan. In the 1960s, only 10 per cent of West Suffolk's new houses were designed by architects. We have come a little way since then, but the SPS committees still see far too many badly drawn-up plans, some by professionals.

The Society's district committees were anxious to establish relations with their local government planning departments right from the start. They were not successful in getting any of their members on to the planning committees, though one or two have district planning officers among their own members. On the whole, relations are easiest between local government councils and SPS committees where communication between them is free and constant. This at least ensures mutual recognition. What had not been foreseen by many people was that few of the members of the new planning departments had any experience of rural districts. Most came from urban or suburban areas, and of those who had been

Suffolk rural districts as they existed from 1888 to 1973.

used to the country, not many were versed in the complex historical character of Suffolk. Some, fortunately, have been interested enough to learn, to attend courses on the landscape or on vernacular architecture, but, as in other human activities, much of the learning is liable to be done by making mistakes; and there is room for stronger representations by the SPS and by the local amenity societies to give help and guidance. Too often there is still a failure to see the landscape (or the townscape) whole.

Changing Relationships

In the years immediately preceding local government reorganization, the links between the SPS and the two county councils had been close, and though there were often differences of opinion, the representatives of the Society on the planning committees were an accepted part of the system of planning policies. With the amalgamation of the county councils and with a much increased number of councillors, it was inevitable that this close relationship had to change. Up until 1976, all the chairmen of the SPS had had links at some time or other with local government, though not necessarily at the time they were in office. Anthony

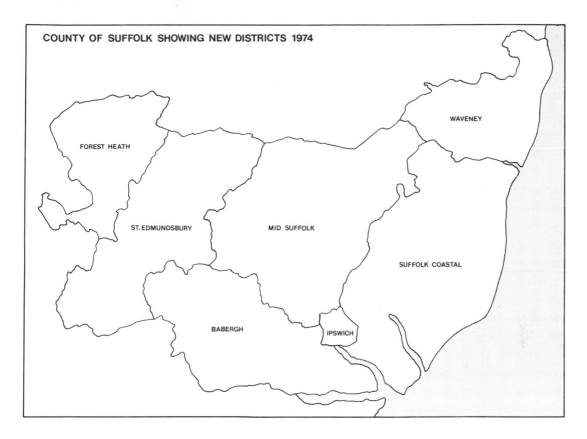

COUNTY OF SUFFOLK SHOWING NEW DISTRICTS 1974

WAVENEY

FOREST HEATH

ST. EDMUNDSBURY

MID SUFFOLK

SUFFOLK COASTAL

BABERGH

IPSWICH

Foord, however, was both Chairman and a member of the County Council simultaneously. There was certainly nothing wrong in this, no reason why a councillor should not have a strong interest in conservation, or why, indeed, this should be considered as anything strange or unusual. During Mr Foord's chairmanship, the Society, under its Director, was becoming more efficient, and was, with its newly formed Finance Committee, able to put its finances on a much more business-like footing. The appointment of Hugh Paget as chairman brought in for the first time someone unconnected with local government who had worked with the British Council and whose interests were mainly historical and visual. While there was no conscious severance on this account from local government, the Society was in fact, with growing experience, learning to pursue its avowed objectives with greater independence and to develop a professionalism of its own. Certain differences of approach are from time to time inevitable between public officials and the executives of an amenity society, and to understand them is to increase rather than diminish the possibilities of effective co-operation.

County Structure Plan

With this new professionalism came many improvements in the casework of the Society. The year 1976 brought the first steps towards the new *County Structure Plan*, the County Council's consultation document on the broad policies that

A long and complicated fight by the SPS to save Glemsford Silk Mill resulted in defeat.

should be laid down for development over the following fifteen years. Naturally, housing, employment and communications were some of the issues under discussion, with new policies for the built-up areas of towns and villages; but, for the first time, conservation of the environment, recreation and tourism were considered as vitally important topics. Since the population in Suffolk had grown from 446,000 in 1961 to 517,000 in 1970 – a rate of growth well above the national average – the Society paid particular attention to the County Council's response to central government's requirements on planning for population growth. The GLC's overspill agreements had yet to be fully carried out, and there was still every indication that Suffolk was continuing to attract large numbers of people who wished to move in from choice.

The SPS's response to the *Written Statement on the Structure Plan* shows a new approach. With the Director's advice that the Society should endeavour to influence county policy at an early stage, it was no longer possible to remain quite so aloof from the political, economic and social questions which have so much bearing on the present-day environment. For the first time, the Society made definite recommendations on the projections for population growth, asking the County Council to limit the figure to approximately 58,000 (the lowest possible figure postulated by the County) in each of the next two decades, instead of the 70,000 suggested. The SPS also asked for termination of 'planned migration', and, subsequently, the GLC sought to terminate this arrangement with the three district councils involved, by mutual agreement.

On conservation matters, the Society was able to put forward suggestions and point out omissions: there was no policy to deal with buildings of architectural and historic importance. In a county with over 10,000 listed buildings, this was a serious matter. Rivers, too, those much neglected and vital features, had been forgotten; they are characteristic and highly vulnerable elements in the landscape and ecology of the county. And, not for the first time, the *Written Statement* put forward the proposition, so often preached and so seldom practised, that new housing should be of a high standard 'which will not detract from the special character of the county'. The Society accordingly put in a strong plea for a design guide for new housing which would reflect the local building tradition. The Minister's decision on the *Structure Plan* has recently been announced, and it may fairly be claimed that the Society was, at least in part, responsible for his selection of the lower set of figures for population projections. In addition, the Society has succeeded in obtaining many minor additions and amendments to proposed policies, particularly those relating to conservation.

These primary issues are of enormous importance to the general development of Suffolk, but, to the ordinary SPS member, they are rather bewildering and technical. What interests most people are the smaller battles, and, with the coming of the district committees, there were plenty of those. The quarterly newsletter advocated by the Director was found to be impractical, but the new editor, Dorothy Goslett, later to take over the office of Hon. Secretary, has, since 1975, produced three times a year a new-style document full of photographs and detailed information of all that is happening around the county. In the pages of this newsletter appeared two recurring cases, one a success story, and one a failure. Both had to do with mills.

The Mills

Glemsford Silk Mill

The saga of Glemsford Silk Mill makes sorry reading. It was a large Victorian red-brick block, built in the early nineteenth century when silk weaving brought some prosperity back to south-west Suffolk. The SPS considered it an important building historically and saw that, with careful internal alteration, it would make admirable accommodation for families or for some cottage industry. The owners were anxious to demolish it and redevelop the site. When permission to demolish was refused by Babergh District Council, the owner appealed to the Secretary of State to reverse the decision. After a public inquiry, at which J. B. Weller and E. Field Reid appeared for the SPS, the owners lost the case. Some months later, fire

In 1978, the Suffolk Preservation Society became the owner of Pakenham Water Mill.

broke out which severely damaged one wing, though the central portion of the mill remained largely intact. Subsequently, the owners reapplied for consent to demolish the building and, in spite of the Society's efforts, the Secretary of State decided to grant consent, without holding a further inquiry.

Pakenham Water Mill

The parish of Pakenham is unique in Britain. It is the only one which still retains a windmill and a watermill, both in working order. The present watermill was built in the eighteenth century, perhaps on the same site as the mill mentioned in Domesday Book. Much of the working machinery belonging to it is between a hundred and two hundred years old. In 1974, the owner wished to retire and to convert the building into a dwelling. Not only would this have meant the removal of the machinery, but there would have been considerable change to the exterior. The SPS managed to persuade the St Edmundsbury District Council to put off its decision on the planning application while it gathered its forces together. More than a year was given to negotiations and enlisting support, during which the help of the SPAB and the Science Museum, was obtained. The SPS was then ready to

The exterior restoration of Pakenham Mill almost complete.

face the public inquiry which the owner had by this time asked for. Thanks largely to the findings of an inspector with expert knowledge of industrial archaeology, the inquiry resulted in the saving of the mill, which finally came into the Society's keeping. Had it not been for generous grants from the Historic Buildings Council, the Science Museum and the county and district councils and, above all, the gift of yet another of the Society's anonymous benefactors, coupled with the fact that the owner accepted a lower price, there would have been no hope of acquiring Pakenham Water Mill. It was a satisfying achievement for the Society in its golden jubilee year to be restoring such an outstanding monument of the rural archaeology of Suffolk. It has always been intended that the public should be able to see the mill not simply as a relic, but as a working and productive building.

Suffolk Heritage Trust

However gratifying the purchase of such a property may be, and however many such purchases may be made in the future, there is no escaping the fact that Suffolk at large is still threatened, not only by the expansion of settlement and

Pakenham water mill, interior.

industry, but by the deterioration and destruction of many of its finest buildings and natural features. The SPS, with its parallel organization, the Suffolk Historic Churches Trust, agreed that a concerted fund-raising drive should be made under the auspices of a special trust for the maintenance of the county's heritage. On a basis of £1 per head of the population the members of the Suffolk Heritage Trust, as it was named, suggested at their inaugural meeting a target of £500,000. The new Trust was to comprise, for the purposes of this operation, the SPS, the Suffolk Historic Churches Trust and the Suffolk Building Preservation Trust. It was subsequently agreed to modify the target to £100,000 for the immediate future, while keeping the larger sum in view. In the first eighteen months, £60,000 was raised; and further avenues still remain to be explored. There are signs that interest in the task of preserving the amenity and beauty of Suffolk is growing in the trades and businesses that owe much of their success to the county.

Membership

The membership of the Society is still only 2,000, out of a total population of 500,000. By national standards this is a high membership figure for a county society, coming somewhere in the top twenty; but it cannot possibly reflect the number of people who care for Suffolk, or the growing numbers of young people

122

who take a passionate interest in conservation. It may be that many of the young are a little wary of established amenity societies; or that the word 'preservation' sounds faintly fusty to their ears, though this is a point members of the society are alive to. When, in 1970, the Council for the Preservation of Rural England changed its name by substituting 'Protection' for 'Preservation', there were many in the SPS who pressed for a change of their own Society's name. 'The Suffolk Society' was suggested, but turned down, mainly because the initials were then thought to have a sinister ring. Perhaps not a very serious objection; the Norfolk Society, for instance, is never known by its initials.

In an effort to attract the younger generation, a reduced subscription has been introduced for members under twenty-five; a close connection has been established with the Suffolk Conservation Corps; and a programme of lectures and practical activities is going forward to encourage interest in the schools.

However, there are many people, often those who join village amenity societies with enthusiasm, who cannot be persuaded to join the larger body. This could be partly a result of expense, though not entirely, for the membership has gone up steadily in spite of inevitable increases in subscription.

The main problem seems to be that of identifying oneself with a unit as large as a county. In this context, detail is easier to understand than the whole; a village is more easily intelligible than a large area. This is an attitude which may be natural to the modern rootless generation who, because of the conditions of their work, tend to lead a nomadic existence. Perhaps the SPS can never hope to capture them in large numbers and must be content with those who expect to spend most of their lives in Suffolk. It is too much to ask for real allegiance to the county from those who see no prospect of settling permanently.

The Long Shop at Garretts' old works site in Leiston which is to become a steam and industrial museum. Originally promoted by SPS, a trust is being formed to manage the project.

9 Conclusion

Suffolk is still an agricultural county. It is natural therefore that the Society should, in recent years, have tried to maintain close contacts with the official representatives of farming, meeting the National Farmers' Union and the Country Landowners' Association on various committees, and itself organizing in May 1979, with the Cambridge University Board of Extra-Mural Studies, a well-attended conference on farm buildings. These are essential steps to better understanding, but they are at the moment only reaching those who are already sympathetically inclined towards conservation. The farmers who are going to be difficult to reach are the kind represented in recent interviews with a random sample of farmers in forty-four parishes of East Suffolk, carried out for the Countryside Commission as part of a survey of farmers' attitudes to conservation by the Department of Sociology at the University of Essex. This sample appears to demonstrate that many farmers, while acknowledging the existence of environmental problems caused by modern farming methods, show a certain hostility to conservationists. If the attitudes expressed by such farmers are correctly interpreted, it seems likely that they will pay little attention either to the SPS or perhaps even to the circulars sent out by the Countryside Commission, the National Farmers' Union and the Country Landowners' Association. The clash of interests between farmers and conservationists may well offer, in the next few years, one of the more difficult problems that the SPS will have to deal with.

Of course, it is always much easier to destroy than to create. Everyone knows the things he most dislikes about new buildings, the shallow-pitched roof when he is used to the steep pitch originally needed for thatch of a timber-framed house; the 'picture window' of ten years ago; the strangely blank look of a house without a chimney (though that would have been natural, after all, in medieval times). But even more depressing than these, perhaps, are the pretentious adjuncts to unassuming cottages; everyone has his own special aversion – John Betjeman's detested carriage lamps; the white-painted cartwheel; the sugar-pink emulsion paint replacing the old luminous lime-wash; the mass-produced bow window with its bogus bottle glass. (Nothing new in disliking this: General Tilney in *Northanger Abbey* – 'between ourselves, if there is one thing more than another my aversion, it is a patched-on bow'.) Though it is unkind to be severe on such things – they after all represent somebody's ideal of rural life – there is no doubt that, with the use of modern pigment for colouring paint and the mass-production of 'Tudor-style' doors, the Suffolk village has lost that unselfconscious charm that it had twenty years ago. One scarcely ever sees now that comfortable shabbiness that comes with a peaceful and, above all, settled existence.

But there is little doubt that, during the next half-century, the SPS, together with all other amenity societies of the same importance, will have to respond to much wider issues. In the past, the voluntary societies have been responsible for

The model of The Suffolk Building Preservation Trust's proposed development at Wetherden. (Architect: David Luckhurst of Feilden & Mawson.)

bringing into existence nearly all the official national bodies. Before the end of this century, it may be vital to consider questions relating to the whole environment, not simply the protection of the countryside – the sympathetic planning of towns, the restoration of buildings and their imaginative re-use in a changing world. Amenity societies may need to be able to decide on their attitudes to energy, transport and pollution; their members may have to work harder to understand and combat the dangers that new technology may bring to the regions they love and whose character they may wish to retain. Here is the opportunity to bring about a more perceptive understanding of the county's inheritance. It is now that the groundwork is being laid on which a new generation of 'professional inhabitants' will build for the next fifty years in the history of Suffolk.

126

Cottages at Boyton: rural simplicity at risk. Mass-produced bow windows and doors with integral fanlights often now replace the originals.

Martlesham New Village: a brave attempt to solve the problem of suitable new housing on a new estate. The effect is uncomfortably cramped, and the lack of chimneys on such traditional houses is disturbing.

Suffolk Coastal District Council was the first Suffolk local authority to set up a revolving fund for the renovation and sale of historic buildings. The Angel Inn, Saxmundham, converted into six houses and a shop.

Earthfield Lane: the medieval highroad from Bury to Ipswich with its ditches, hedges and pollards intact. The SPS made strong representation to the Department of the Environment, emphasizing its historic and environmental importance, but nearly all of it has now disappeared under the new alignment of the A45.

Signposts like this one at Bungay, and even the simpler finger-posts, may eventually disappear to be replaced by the standard signs used on major roads.

Bricks and tiles were made by hand for over a hundred years at Cove Bottom Brickworks. In 1976 the works were closed down and the buildings threatened with demolition. The following year they were back in production.

Fine quality iron-work at Felixstowe's redundant station. The Felixstowe Society are anxious to find a new use for the building in order to save it from demolition.

Snape Maltings: one of the finest concert halls in Europe, set in idyllic marshland. A magnificent conversion of an obsolete industrial building.

Small houses like these, unlisted and outside Conservation Areas, cannot be protected from sympathetic replacement of doors and windows.

133

An enjoyable introduction to responsibility. Conservation will soon be in the hands of these children.

Appendix One

The Officers of the SPS from Its Foundation

PATRON:	Commander the Earl of Stradbroke, RN	(from 1957)
PRESIDENT:	Viscount Ullswater, PC, GCB	1929–40
	Sir John Tilley, PC, GCMG, GCVO	1940–52
	The Earl of Stradbroke	1953–57
	The Earl of Euston	
	(now the Duke of Grafton, KG)	1957–
CHAIRMAN:	William Rowley Elliston, DL	1929–53
	The Earl of Stradbroke	1953–56
	F. H. A. Engleheart	1956–63
	Sir Joshua Rowley, Bt.	1963–67
	Sir William Bunbury, Bt.	1967–70
	Henry Engleheart	1970–73
	Anthony Foord	1973–76
	Hugh Paget, CBE	1976–79
	Desmond Pakenham, CBE	1979–
HON. SECRETARY:	Mrs Elmer Schofield	1929–37
	The Rev. (now Canon) W. M. Lummis, MC	1937–47
	Seymour Schofield	1947–50
	F. Bridgeman	1950–53
	F. G. M. Westropp	1956–66
	Henry Engleheart (acting)	1966–67
	E. Field Reid	1967–75
	Miss Dorothy Goslett	1975–
HON. TREASURER:	Mrs Elmer Schofield	1929–37
	F. H. Smith	1937–43
	The Rev. (now Canon) W. M. Lummis, MC	1943–47
	Seymour Schofield	1947–50
	F. Bridgeman, Noel Turner and others	1950–57
	F. J. Watt	1957–62
	R. Blenkinsopp	1962–73
	E. T. Knott	1973–74
	E. P. Arundell	1974–76
	G. M. Murray	1977
	A. L. Evans	1977–79
	Ray Hardingham	1979–
HON. MEMBERSHIP SECRETARY:	George Coulson	1971–79
	J. W. L. Shillidy	1979–
DIRECTOR:	J. H. Popham, FRICS	1974–
	(full-time salaried appointment)	

Appendix Two

The Officers of the SPS in 1930

President

The Viscount Ullswater, PC, GCB

Vice-presidents

The Lord Bishop of St Edmundsbury and Ipswich
The Lord Henniker
Sir Robert Shafto Adair, Bt.
F. G. Clavering Fison, MP
Brigadier-General Lord Playfair, CVO, TD, DL
Montague Rendall, MA, LlD
Rev. Edmund Farrer, FSA
The Worshipful the Mayor of Ipswich
Sir John Ganzoni, MP
Sir Cuthbert Quilter, Bt.
V. B. Redstone, FSA, FH Hist.
Bernard Corder

Chairman: Major Rowley Elliston, MA, DL

Hon. Secretary: Mrs Elmer Schofield

There is no complete list of the earliest committee. During 1930, the following attended one or more committee meetings. Those marked with an asterisk seem to have attended nearly all the meetings.

Colonel Bond
Sir Arthur Churchman
H. N. Collinson
Rev. G. H. Lenox Conyngham*
E. R. Cooper
Rev. Edmund Farrer*
The Hon. Mrs Douglas Hamilton
Rev. H. Harris
Rev. H. Copinger Hill*
General Kenyon*
Harold Lingwood*
Miss Hilda Mason*
Guy Maynard
John Muriel
R. C. Notcutt*
Canon A. F. Northcote
E. D. Nuttall*
Cecil Oakes*
Charles Partridge*
Colonel W. G. Carwardine Probert
F. Lingard Ranson
V. B. Redstone*

Dr Montague Rendall
Mrs Arthur Sherston*
F. H. Smith*
The Hon. Mrs Douglas Tollemache
J. E. Wedgwood
Haydn Whitehead*

Appendix Three

Suffolk County Organizations

1853	The Suffolk Institute of Archaeology and Natural History
1929	The Suffolk Naturalists' Society
1929	The Suffolk Preservation Society
1958	The Suffolk Records Society
1961	The Suffolk Trust for Nature Conservation
1973	Suffolk Building Preservation Trust Ltd
1973	Suffolk Committee, Farming and Wildlife Advisory Group
1974	Suffolk Historic Churches Trust
1975	Suffolk Conservation Corps
1975	The Suffolk Buildings Recording Group
1977	The Suffolk Mills Group

Appendix Four

Amenity Societies in Suffolk

	Date of foundation	Number of members as at 1 November 1979
Dedham Vale Society	1938	214
Lavenham Preservation Society	1944	Approx. 30 life members
Woodbridge Society	1951 (reconstituted)	160
Cavendish Preservation Society*	1955 (reconstituted 1972)	–
The Ipswich Society	1960	470
Pin Mill Preservation Society	1964	99
Beccles Society	1966	145
Eastern Federation of Amenity Societies	1966	29 societies in Suffolk, Norfolk, Essex and Cambridge
Needham Market Society	1966	61
Colne/Stour Countryside Association	1969	210
Aldeburgh Society	1970	580
Bungay Society	1971	109
Bury St Edmunds Society	1971	384
East Bergholt Society	1972	256
Sudbury Society	1972	104
Boxford Society	1973	160
Nayland-with-Wissington Conservation Society	1974	157
Southwold and Reydon Society (successor to Southwold and Reydon Residents' Association)	1974	509
Little Cornard Conservation Society	1976	35
Stowmarket Society	1976	35
Felixstowe Society	1978	60
Hadleigh and District Residents and Conservation Association	1978	112

*Registered with the Civic Trust, but currently having no members.

Appendix Five

Bodies on which the SPS has Official Representation

The Society has official representation on the committees or panels of the following bodies:

Alton Water Amenities Consultative Panel
Anglian Water Authority: River Stour Users Consultative Panel for Recreation and Amenity
Association for Suffolk Museums
Best Kept Village Committee of the Community Council for Suffolk
Broads Consultative Committee
Community Council for Suffolk: Executive Committee
Council for British Archaeology: Group VI
Council for the Protection of Rural England: Executive and Finance and General Purposes
    Committees
Dedham Vale Countryside Centre
Farming & Wildlife Advisory Group: Suffolk Committee
Ipswich Conservation Advisory Panel
Suffolk Association of Local Councils
Suffolk Building Preservation Trust
Suffolk Heritage Trust
Suffolk Historic Churches Trust
Suffolk Local History Council of the Community Council for Suffolk
Suffolk New Agricultural Landscapes Project: Advisory Committee

Appendix Six

Some Landmarks in the Development of Conservation

1791   *Ordnance Survey* founded; mapping of England and Wales, primarily for defence but the foundation for future recording of natural and historic features.

*1865   *Commons Preservation Society* (now Commons, Open Spaces and Footpaths Preservation Society).

1873   *National Monuments Preservation Bill* unsuccessfully introduced by Sir John Lubbock.

*1877   *Society for the Protection of Ancient Buildings* founded by William Morris.

1882   *Ancient Monuments Protection Act*: first scheduling of 21 ancient monuments including Stonehenge. Extended 1913, 1931, 1937 and 1943.

*1889   *Society for the Protection of Birds* (now Royal Society for the Protection of Birds).

*1895   *National Trust for Places of Historic Interest and Natural Beauty*: to hold land and property for the benefit of the nation: incorporated by Act of Parliament in 1907.

*1899   *Garden City Association* (now the Town and Country Planning Association).

*1900   *Victoria County History Series* begun. Recent volumes have been published under the auspices of the Institute of Historical Research.

1908–10   *Royal Commission on Historical Monuments*: founded for England, Scotland and Wales.

1909   *Housing and Town Planning Act*.

1913   *Ancient Monuments Consolidation Act*: first statutory preservation powers on scheduled monuments.

*1914   *Town Planning Institute*.

1919   *Housing and Town Planning Act*: planning schemes obligatory for all towns and boroughs with population exceeding 20,000.

*1922   *Men of the Trees Society*.

*1922   *Central Council for Care of Churches*.

*1924   *Ancient Monuments Society*.

1925   *Housing and Town Planning Act*.

*1926   *Council for the Preservation of Rural England* ('Preservation' became 'Protection' in 1969).

1932   *Town and Country Planning Act*: first mention of rural planning and first powers over inhabited buildings.

1935   *Restriction of Ribbon Development Act*.

*1937   *Georgian Group*.

*1939   *Central Council of Civic Societies*.

1943   *Minister of Town and Country Planning Act*: established Ministry and laid down its functions.

1944   *Town and Country Planning Act*: gave urban authorities powers of requisition and re-planning and authorized compilation of lists of buildings of historic and architectural interest.

1947   *Town and Country Planning Act*: zoning of land for housing, industry, recreation, etc., compulsory development plans to be revised every five years.

1947   *Nature Conservancy Council*.

1949   *National Parks and Access to the Countryside Act*: designation of National Parks and Areas of Outstanding Natural Beauty.

1950   *The Gowers Report*: committee of inquiry into the state of historic houses.

1951   *Minister of Local Government and Planning (change of style and title) Order*: superseded Ministry of Town and Country Planning.

1953	*Historic Buildings and Acient Monuments Act*: set up Historic Buildings Council for furthering the preservation of houses of outstanding historic or architectural interest with expert advice, grants, etc.
*1957	*Civic Trust* superseded the Central Council of Civic Societies.
*1958	*Victorian Society.*
*1963	*Europa Nostra*: federation of several thousand amenity societies in twenty European countries.
1967	*Civic Amenities Act*: established criteria for Conservation Areas.
*1967	*Conservation Society.*
1968	*National Parks Commission* became *Countryside Commission.*
1970	*The Secretary of State for the Environment Order*: establishment of the Department of the Environment.
*1970	*Friends of the Earth*: inspired from the USA.
1970	*European Conservation Year.*
1972	*National Buildings Record* became *National Monuments Record.*
*1974	*European Environmental Bureau*: international organization dealing with conservation within the framework of the EEC.
1974	*Town and Country Planning Amenities Act*: improved support for conservation.
1975	*European Architectural Heritage Year.*

*Voluntary and independent bodies and organizations.

West Stow Hall.

Appendix Seven

Suffolk Houses Destroyed, 1890–1961

1890	Hurts Hall, Saxmundham (NH, 1893)
c.1914	Barton Hall (F)
1923	Livermere Hall
1924	Easton Park
1926	Hardwick House, Bury St Edmunds
1930	Oakley Park
1934	Mildenhall Manor
c.1935	Red House, Ipswich
1941	Carlton Hall (F)
1949	Cavenham Hall
1949	Rendlesham Hall
c.1949	Thorington Hall
c.1950	Bredfield White House
1950	Moulton Paddock House
1952	Edwardstone Hall
1953	High House, Campsea Ashe
1953	Drinkstone Hall
1953	Flixton Hall
1953	Henham Hall
1953	Rougham Hall
1953	Sudbourne Hall
1953	Theberton Manor
1953	Ufford Place
1955	Bramford Park
1955	Chediston Hall
c.1955	Fornham Hall
1955	Ousden Hall
1955	Thistleton Hall, Burgh
1955	Wamil Hall, Mildenhall (PD)
1957	Assington Hall (F)
c.1958	Boulge Hall
c.1959	Branches Park, Cowlinge
c.1959	Brome Hall
1960	Redgrave Hall
1960	Tendring Hall, Stoke-by-Nayland
1961	Rushbrooke Hall

Key: PD = Partial demolition.
    F = Fire.
    NH = New home on site.

Revised from the list in Roy Strong, Marcus Binney and John Harris, *The Destruction of the Country House 1875–1975*, Thames & Hudson, London, 1976.

Appendix Eight

Chronological List of Suffolk Plans and Surveys

1935	East Suffolk	Regional planning scheme prepared for the East Suffolk Joint Regional Planning Committee	Abercrombie & Kelly
1942	Lowestoft	Report of the main factors to be considered in the preparation of the preliminary planning scheme (typescript)	Lowestoft Corporation
1944	Lavenham	Survey and report for Cosford RDC (typescript)	SPAB and SPS
1945–6	Ipswich	Plan for Ipswich (Housing and Town Planning Committee)	Ipswich Corporation
1946	Suffolk	Suffolk planning survey prepared for the ESCC and the WSCC Joint Planning Committee	County Planning Officer
1946	Ipswich	Plan for the development of the town (typescript)	Communist Party of Ipswich
1948	Lowestoft	Factual survey (typescript)	ESCC
1948	Southwold	Factual survey (typescript)	ESCC
1949	Lowestoft	Outline plan: interim report (typescript)	ESCC
1949	Lowestoft	Interim report on outline development plan (typescript)	Lowestoft Corporation
1949	Sudbury	A full life in the country: the Sudbury and district survey and plan	K. Jeremiah
1950	East Suffolk	Preliminary report on the outline plan for East Suffolk (typescript)	ESCC
1950	Beccles	Survey and outline plan	ESCC
1950	Lowestoft	Outline plan	ESCC
1951	East Suffolk	County development plan: written statement and maps for the county, Lowestoft, Beccles, Woodbridge and 22 designation maps (typescript)	ESCC
1951	West Suffolk	County development plan: written statement, Bury St Edmunds	WSCC
1951	Bury St Edmunds	Factual survey and outline plan	WSCC
1951	Woodbridge	Factual survey and outline plan for the Urban District of Woodbridge (typescript)	ESCC

1953	Felixstowe	Factual survey and outline plan	ESCC
1953	Newmarket	Factual survey and outline plan for the Urban District of Newmarket	WSCC
1954	West Suffolk	County map: written statement	WSCC
1954	Ipswich	Town map: written statement	ESCC
1954	Ipswich	Development plan (typescript)	Ipswich Corporation
1954	Stowmarket	Factual survey and outline plan (typescript)	ESCC
1955	Lothingland NE	Factual survey and outline plan	ESCC
1956	East Suffolk	County plan: Ipswich	ESCC
1956	Bury St Edmunds	The question and the answer (opportunities for industrialists)	Bury St Edmunds Corporation
1956	Haverhill	Factual survey and outline plan	WSCC
1957	Stowmarket	County development plan: Amendment No. 2	ESCC
1958	West Suffolk	Development control notes	WSCC
1958	Bury St Edmunds	Opportunity for industry	Bury St Edmunds Corporation
1958	Newmarket	Town map: written statement	WSCC
1959	East Suffolk	Planning for developments: SW Deben and villages round Ipswich. Factual survey and outline plan	ESCC
1959	Framlingham	Factual survey and outline plan	ESCC
1959	Ipswich	Development plan: report of survey (Town and Country Planning Act 1947)	Ipswich Corporation
1960	Aldeburgh	Outline plan	ESCC
1960	Bury St Edmunds	Central area redevelopment proposals	Bury St Edmunds Development Committee
1960	Lowestoft	Lowestoft amenity improvement schemes	Tayler & Green (arch.)
1961	East Suffolk	County map: written statement	ESCC
1961	Bury St Edmunds	Report on the Corn Exchange for the Borough Council (typescript)	Tayler & Green (arch.)
1961	Haverhill	Joint technical report	WSCC, GLC and Ministry of Housing and Local Government
1961	Ipswich	Town map: written statement	ESCC
1961	Lavenham	Lavenham past – present – future. Report prepared for the county of West Suffolk and Cosford RDC	D. W. Insall
1961	Lavenham	Buildings of architectural and historic interest	WSCC
1961	Leiston	Factual survey and outline plan	ESCC
1961	Southwold	Factual survey and outline plan	ESCC

1962	East Suffolk	Ipswich regional plan: survey and analysis	ESCC
1962	West Suffolk	County development plan: first review, report of survey	WSCC
1962	Bury St Edmunds	Town map	WSCC
1962	Halesworth	Factual survey and outline plan	ESCC
1962	Ipswich	Development plan: written statement (Town and Country Planning Act 1962)	Ipswich Corporation
1962	Sudbury	Outline planning proposals (typescript)	WSCC
1963	Capel St Mary	Factual survey and outline plan	ESCC
1963	Felixstowe	Town map: report of survey and analysis	ESCC
1963	Haverhill	First review	WSCC
1964	South-East England	South-east study 1961–81	Ministry of Housing and Local Government
1964	East Suffolk	The Government's south-east study 1961–81: a report by the Chief Planning Officer	ESCC
1964	West Suffolk	Villages of outstanding importance	WSCC
1964	Bury St Edmunds	Bury St Edmunds cathedral close: landscape report (typescript)	S. Crowe & Associates
1964	Belton	Outline plan	ESCC
1964	Ipswich	A planning study for town development: a report to the Ministry of Housing and Local Government (typescript)	L. G. Vincent and R. Gorking
1964	Lowestoft	Central area: survey and appraisal	ESCC
1964	Sudbury	Factual survey and outline plan for Sudbury, Chilton and Cornard, including town expansion proposals	WSCC
1965	East Suffolk	County development plan: policy for the classification of settlements (2nd edn, 1969)	ESCC
1965	Eastern Region	Social and economic survey	Labour Party Eastern Regional Council
1965	Bury St Edmunds	Town map: written statement	WSCC
1965	Hadleigh	Factual survey and outline plan for the Urban District of Hadleigh	WSCC
1965	Lowestoft	Lowestoft central area draft plan	ESCC
1965	Newmarket	No. 2 CDA map: written statement	WSCC
1965	Sudbury	Sudbury, Chilton and Cornard town map: first review	WSCC
1966	Dedham Vale	Dedham Vale, part 1: Survey and report; part 2: Proposals 1968	Essex and West and East Suffolk County Councils
1966	Beccles	Survey and appraisal	ESCC (Townscape survey based on work by SPS)

146

1966	Bury St Edmunds	Redevelopment proposals for part of the town centre	WSCC
1966	Haverhill	People in Haverhill	WSCC
1966	Ipswich	Expansion of Ipswich: designation proposals, consultants study of the town in its sub-region: a report for the Ministry of Housing and Local Government	Shankland, Cox & Associates
1966	Ipswich	Report by the Chief Planning Officer on the Shankland, Cox report on Ipswich expansion	ESCC
1966	Lowestoft	Town centre map	ESCC
1966	Newmarket	Town map	WSCC
1966	Sudbury, Chilton and Cornard	Town map: written statement	WSCC
1966	Woodbridge	Survey and appraisal: with parts of Deben Rural District	ESCC (Townscape survey based on work by SPS)
1967	East Anglia	Growth and change – East Anglia	East Anglia Economic Planning Council
1967	East Anglia	Regional planning and East Anglia: report of the proceedings of the first annual conference	East Anglian Regional Studies Group
1967	East Suffolk	Policy for conservation areas	ESCC
1967	South-East England	A strategy for the south-east	South-East Economic Planning Council
1967	West Suffolk	Trees: countryside sub-committee report	WSCC
1967	Beccles	Town map: written statement: with part of Wainford Rural District	ESCC
1967	Eye	Policy statement and planning proposals	ESCC
1967	Ipswich	Supplementary report by the Chief Planning Officer on the Shankland, Cox report	ESCC
1968	East Anglia	Eastern area: East of England, a Tory study	Conservative and Unionist Party
1968	East Anglia	East Anglia, a regional study	East Anglian Consultative Committee
1968	East Anglia	East Anglia, a study: a first report of the East Anglia Economic Planning Council	East Anglia Economic Planning Council
1968	West Suffolk	Rural Planning in West Suffolk	WSCC
1968	Beccles	Town centre map	ESCC
1968	Bury St Edmunds	No. 1 CDA map: written statement	WSCC
1968	East Bergholt	Policy statement and planning proposals	ESCC
1968	Felixstowe	Appraisal	ESCC
1968	Hadleigh	Town map	WSCC

1968	Hadleigh	Conservation area no. 1	WSCC
1968	Holbrook	Policy statement and planning proposals	ESCC
1968	Hopton (Lowestoft)	Policy statement and planning proposals	ESCC
1968	Ipswich	Draft Ipswich New Town (designation) order, explanatory memorandum (New Town Act 1965) (typescript)	Ministry of Housing and Local Government
1968	Ipswich	Draft basic plan. Consultants' proposals for the expanded town. Report to the Ministry of Housing and Local Government and Ipswich Borough Council	Shankland, Cox & Associates
1968	Ipswich	Expansion of Ipswich, comparative costs: a supplementary report to the Ministry of Housing and Local Government	Shankland, Cox & Associates
1968	Ipswich	Proposed expansion of Ipswich. Report of chairman of County Planning Committee	ESCC
1968	Newmarket	No. 3 CDA map: written statement	
1968	Stowmarket	Report of survey and appraisal: with parts of Gipping Rural District	ESCC
1968	Walsham-le-Willows	Buildings of Walsham-le-Willows (S. Colman)	WSCC
1968	Woodbridge	Town map: with parts of Deben Rural District	ESCC
1968	Woolpit	Buildings of Woolpit (S. Colman)	WSCC
1969	East Anglia	Government reply to the East Anglia Economic Planning Council's East Anglia study	Department of Economic Affairs
1969	Bury St Edmunds	Bury St Edmunds and town expansion	Bury St Edmunds Corporation
1969	Eye	Conservation in Eye	ESCC
1969	Hadleigh	A townscape analysis (typescript)	Eastern Federation of Amenity Societies
1969	Mildenhall	Plan	WSCC
1969	Sudbury	Report of survey (typescript)	SPS
1970	Bungay	Conservation in Bungay	ESCC
1970	Bury St Edmunds	Town expansion and you	Bury St Edmunds Corporation
1970	Bury St Edmunds	Breckland area scheme	WSCC
1970	Felixstowe	Town map: written statement. Town centre map	ESCC
1970	Halesworth	Policy statement and planning proposals. Town centre map	ESCC
1970	Ipswich	Ipswich fringe area: interim planning statement	ESCC and Ipswich Corporation
1970	Kessingland	Policy statement and planning proposals: village and coast	ESCC

1970	Needham Market	Conservation in Needham Market: townscape appraisal and policy statement	ESCC
1970	Stowmarket	Town map and town centre map: with parts of Gipping Rural District	ESCC
1970	Stowmarket	Town centre map	ESCC
1970	SW. Deben	Policy statement and planning proposals	ESCC
1971	Haverhill	Master plan	WSCC
1971	Hollesley	Village plan	ESCC
1971	Kedington	Village plan	WSCC
1971	Lowestoft	Town map	ESCC
1971	Needham Market	Policy statement and planning proposals	ESCC
1972	Beccles	Town map: written statement	ESCC
1972	Bury St Edmunds	Town development	WSCC
1972	Debenham	Policy statement and planning proposals	ESCC
1972	Felixstowe	Town map: written statement	ESCC
1972	Framlingham	Conservation in Framlingham	ESCC
1972	Grundisburgh	Village plan	ESCC
1972	Lavenham	Conservation and village plan	WSCC
1972	Hadleigh	Draft town map	WSCC
1972	Thurston	Village plan	WSCC
1972	Framlingham	Policy statement and planning proposals	ESCC
1973	Barrow	Village plan	WSCC
1973	Boxford	Village plan	WSCC
1973	Elmswell	Village plan	WSCC
1973	Freckenham	Village plan	WSCC
1973	Glemsford	Village plan	WSCC
1973	Lakenheath	Village plan	WSCC
1973	Long Melford	Village plan	WSCC
1973	Otley	Village plan	WSCC
1973	Stanton	Village plan	WSCC
1973	Walsham-le-Willows	Village plan	WSCC
1973	Woolpit	Village plan	WSCC
1974	East Anglia	Strategic choice for East Anglia	East Anglia Strategy Team
1974	Bildeston	Village plan	Suffolk CC
1974	Brandon	Plan	Suffolk CC
1974	Clare	Village plan	Suffolk CC
1974	Ixworth	Village plan	Suffolk CC
1975	Suffolk	Development plan scheme	Suffolk CC

1975	Suffolk	The choice ahead. The next steps	Suffolk CC
1975	Haverhill	Town map: written statement	Suffolk CC
1975	Peasenhall	Peasenhall and Sibton appraisal and policy statement	Suffolk Coastal DC
1975	Stowmarket	Town map: written statement	Suffolk CC
1976	Aldeburgh	Consultative document for public discussion	The Aldeburgh Society
1976	East Anglia	East Anglia regional strategy: government response to strategic choice	Department of the Environment
1976	Suffolk	Suffolk: the next 15 years	Suffolk CC
1976	Gislingham	Village plan	Mid Suffolk DC
1976	Great Finborough	Village plan	Mid Suffolk DC
1976	Haughley	Village plan	Mid Suffolk DC
1976	Newmarket	District plan	Forest Heath DC
1976	Wickham Market	Appraisal and policy statement: Wickham Market, Ufford and Pettistree	Suffolk Coastal District Council
1976	Woodbridge	Conservation in Woodbridge	Suffolk CC
1976	Suffolk	Suffolk county – structure plan: written statement (consultation draft)	Suffolk CC
1977	Beyton	Village study	Mid Suffolk DC
1977	Wangford	Village plan	Waveney DC
1978	Dedham Vale	Landscape study	Suffolk and Essex CCs with Colchester BC and Babergh DC
1978	Framlingham	Issues report	Suffolk Coastal DC
1978	Gipping Valley	Gipping valley plan	Suffolk CC with Babergh and Mid Suffolk CC
1978	Leiston	Issues report	Suffolk Coastal CC
1978	Sudbury	District plan (consultation draft)	Babergh DC
1978	Suffolk Heritage Coast	Plan	Suffolk CC with Suffolk Coastal DC & Waveney DC
1979	Halesworth and Holton	District plan (consultation draft)	Waveney DC
1979	Lowestoft and N. Waveney	District plan (consultation draft)	Waveney DC
1979	Saxmundham and Kelsale	Issues report and by-pass options	Suffolk Coastal DC
1979	Stowmarket	District plan (consultation draft)	Mid Suffolk DC

Appendix Nine

Nature Reserves in Suffolk

1. Nature Conservancy Council National Nature Reserves

Limited open access reserves

Cavenham Heath, Suffolk
(376 acres)

Nature trail and a car park and free access to a limited area of heath. Permits are required for the rest of the reserve and some sections are completely closed during the breeding season.

Orfordness/Havergate
(555 acres)

Havergate Island owned by the RSPB. Permits are required to visit it and are only available on certain days during the week. Orfordness is normally open, but the only access is by boat. Temporary restrictions may be placed on parts of the Ness from time to time.

Walberswick (1,270 acres)

Free access to the public rights of way from which most of the features of the reserve can be appreciated. Permits to visit the rest of the reserve are very strictly rationed and are normally given only to *bona fide* research workers.

Westleton Heath (117 acres)

Free access to the picnic area and to the public footpaths. Permits are available for the remainder of the reserve.

Closed reserves

Thetford Heath (243 acres)

The reserve is closed from April to the end of July. Permits can be obtained for visits outside this period. The reserve is owned by the Norfolk Naturalists' Trust.

2. Suffolk Trust for Nature Conservation

Open reserves

Cornard Mere, Little Cornard
Flixton Holes
Hascot Pit, Battisford
Thelnetham Fen

Reserves with limited access for the general public

Bromeswell Green
Bull's Wood, Cockfield (public right of way through wood)
Fox Fritillary Meadow, Framsden (two days a year for the general public)
Landguard Point, Felixstowe (a statutory Local Nature Reserve)
Newbourn Springs
Potash Lane Hedge, Polstead
Redgrave and Lopham Fens
Sprat's Water, Carlton Colville

Drury's Spinney, Snape
Gromford Meadow, Snape
Groton Wood
High House, Monewden
Lakenheath Poor's Fen
Mickfield Meadow
Pashford Poor's Fen, Lakenheath
Norman Gwatkin Reserve, Henham

Reserves with restricted access even to Trust members

Hollesley Heath
Lady's Mantle Meadow, Cransford
Moat Farm, Otley
Rookery Farm, Monewden
Tuddenham Gallops, Barton Mills
Wangford Glebe

Other STNC reserves

The Rex Graham Reserve, Mildenhall, is open to the public on one day each year but is completely closed at all other times.

3. Royal Society for the Protection of Birds' Reserves

Reserves with restricted access

Havergate Island	See above under Orfordness/Havergate NNR.
Minsmere Bird Reserve	Access by permit, available on site in limited numbers. The reserve is not open every day.
North Warren, Leiston	Nature trail, but the rest of the reserve only open by special arrangement.
Wolves Wood, Hadleigh	Nature trail, but the rest of the reserve only open by special arrangement.

4. Other Owners/Managers

Open reserves

Dunwich Heath, National Trust	Open on payment of entry fee.
Broom Hill, Hadleigh. Babergh District Council Non-Statutory Local Nature Reserve	Open at all times.
Knettishall Heath Country Park.* Suffolk County Council	Open at all times.
Ramparts Field Picnic Area,* Icklingham. Suffolk County Council	Open at all times.
West Stow Country Park,* West Stow. St Edmundsbury District Council	Open at all times.

Bradfield Woods.	Free access along rides.
Society for the Promotion of Nature	Visiting parties need approval.
Conservation	

*Not managed primarily as nature reserves, but nevertheless very important for their wildlife.

Appendix Ten

Planned Migration in Suffolk

Town	Town population 1961	Town Development Act proposals, 1961	Total population 1971	Planned migration to 1971	Total population, 1976	Planned migration 1971–6	Total planned migration to 1976
Bury St Edmunds	21,179	10,000	25,661	3,000	27,630	1,200	4,200
Haverhill	5,447	10,000	12,421	4,900	15,900	2,000	6,900
Sudbury and Great Cornard	9,058	7,000	15,081	2,300	16,930	1,300	3,600
Brandon	3,344	2,000	4,572	200	5,720	450	650
Mildenhall	7,132	5,000	9,269	1,300	11,280	900	2,200

Planned migration figures are based on Suffolk County Council's estimates of migrant population using the number of dwellings occupied, multiplied by an average occupancy rate on initial occupation. Total population figures for 1976 are based on Suffolk County Council's population estimates.

Butley Priory gatehouse.

Appendix Eleven

Notes on Population Changes, 1931–77

The figures in the table below show the increase of population and the relative increase and decrease of population in the parishes of the Suffolk districts since the founding of the Suffolk Preservation Society.

Since the six districts were not created until 1974, the 1931 figures are based on the numbers in individual parishes in the National Census of that year. The 1977 figures are taken from county council population estimates.

In a few cases, the increase/decrease totals are marginal.

In many cases, the rise or decline of village populations is the result of county settlement policy. There are also special circumstances which should be taken into account, as follows:

Babergh: The district includes some villages close enough to London (by rail) or to Ipswich and Colchester to attract commuters. The Sudbury area was part of West Suffolk until 1974 and there has been a large influx of people under the Town Development Agreement Scheme since 1965.

Suffolk Coastal: The growth of Felixstowe is an important element in the population increase. The figures include USAF personnel and their families at Woodbridge Air Base.

Mid Suffolk: Main pressure for development is on the Ipswich fringe area, the Stowmarket area and villages along the A45. Economic decline has affected the northern and north-eastern parts of the district.

Waveney: Parishes close to Lowestoft and the smaller towns have grown substantially, particularly during the 1960s. Agricultural parishes seem to have declined except for those where planning policy is for limited growth.

Forest Heath: Newmarket and its surrounding parishes show substantial increase. USAF personnel and their dependants account for large increases at Mildenhall, Lakenheath and Eriswell.

St Edmundsbury: Town Development Agreement schemes at Bury St Edmunds and Haverhill partly account for the growth in population. Parishes close to the Essex border seem to be declining.

District	Total population 1931	Estimated total population 1977	Total number of parishes	Number and percentage of parishes with population increase since 1931		Number and percentage of parishes with population decrease since 1931	
				No.	%	No.	%
Babergh	44,971	70,530	76	45	59	31	41
Suffolk Coastal	68,609	93,700	117	47	40	70	60
Mid Suffolk	45,832	66,830	123	61	50	62	50
Waveney	76,037	97,300	63	24	38	39	62
Forest Heath	22,082	45,200	20	13	65	7	35
St Edmundsbury	44,816	82,830	83	49	59	34	41

Appendix Twelve

Two Articles from the *East Anglian Magazine* (1936)

Should Old Buildings be Preserved? YES

by MURIEL R. SCHOFIELD
Secretary, Suffolk Preservation Society

From the aesthetic point of view there is an overwhelming body of enlightened public opinion in favour of the retention and preservation of ancient buildings, and most people are unanimous as to their historical, educational and pictorial value.

It is, however, when these values come into opposition with modern progress that the difficulties of preservation become apparent.

Utility and humanitarianism, progress and rights of property, unemployment, and sanitation are then ranged into a formidable array against what appears to be nothing more than a sentimental love of history, beauty, and tradition. But a closer examination of the united front of progress reveals the weakness of this ill-assorted alliance. The Slum Clearance schemes provide a case in point. In the large manufacturing centres they can do nothing but good if properly applied, and in the case of some of the Northern towns, and parts of London, they might with advantage be much more drastic. When, however, these clearances are extended to the smaller towns and country villages, the weakness of the scheme is exposed.

Fine old houses of the Tudor period which, although dilapidated, are sound structurally, are condemned by the surveyors and MO's, as irreparable, and are swept away together with the flimsy brick shacks of Victorian speculators. Road widening and slum clearance are cunningly combined, and clearance sites are devoted to car-parks for the well-to-do shoppers instead of re-housing for the workers. Often the dispossessed slum dwellers are provided with fine new houses far from their place of work, and at greatly increased rentals. Central sites of great value are often built over with detached pairs of country cottages. The greatest absurdity is seen in the large villages or little towns, where groups of cottages, often let at nominal rents to old couples, are swept away without any architectural advice at all. In many cases these old houses and cottages could be reconditioned at considerably less cost than it would take to replace them, and in such cases advice should be obtained from qualified architects who specialize in this type of work. The splendid work done under the guidance of the Society for the Protection of Ancient Buildings all over England, and isolated examples such as the old houses in Norwich repaired by Major Glendinning, show the economy and utility of preservation as against demolition.

If the best of the old houses and cottages were spared it would still be possible to build the same number of new ones, and thus reduce rents, which in the country are far too high for the agricultural labourer to pay. The only way to cope with modern conditions is by comprehensive and compulsory schemes of town and country planning, carried out under professional supervision, and properly co-ordinated. Anti-social activities of speculators would thus be curbed, and the problem of re-housing could be dealt with as a whole. Elevations of new buildings should pass before a County Committee, with a right of appeal to a national body, and in this way we should be spared the horror of mock-Tudor bungalows on the Cornish cliffs. Ancient buildings could be examined by qualified architects, and if economically possible they could be adapted to modern living requirements. In

156

cases where the buildings had definite antiquarian value, but were badly dilapidated, the State might make a grant towards repair.

In this manner the rapid disfigurement of the towns and countryside would be checked – new buildings would be properly designed and sited, and would harmonize in colour and materials with their surroundings. The old house and cottages, reconditioned by means of a subsidy (similar to that under the Rural Workers Housing Act), could be let at low rentals and over-crowding would disappear.

The foregoing remarks have been necessarily brief, but I hope that I have been able to show that there is something more than sentiment behind the idea that, whenever possible, old buildings ought to be retained.

Should Old Buildings be Preserved? NO

by JOHN SUFFOLK

The case against the preservation of the majority of old buildings may be set out like this:

(i)   They are insanitary and unhealthy.
(ii)   They do not blend well with modern architecture.
(iii)   They remind us of a past which is better forgotten.

As to the first point (and please remember I am dealing with the small man's dwelling and not the mansion of the great) – small windows, low ceilings, draughty rooms, ill-fitting doors, sanitation that might have been tolerated centuries ago. Need I catalogue anything more? And they are not beautiful! How can anything be beautiful when it fails to serve the purpose for which it was built? Why spend money rebuilding these places when the same money – plus an architect with vision – will produce something more suited to the times?

Point number two. Recently I saw a new factory which has been built in Ipswich. Its severe lines, the strength of its red brick and the dignity of its white facings were pleasing. 'This,' I said, 'is what 1936 can do.' In another part of the town is a rebuilt shop – rebuilt because its style appealed to the number of those who think things which are old are necessarily good. And it wasn't even upright! Years ago buildings were probably not true because it was beyond the skill of the builders to make them so, but such things are not permissible now.

Point three. History is an absorbing study and the more this study is pursued the more convinced one becomes that now, and only now, are we on the threshold of civilization. I say threshold because humanity stands just as good a chance of falling outside as in. If it does fall outside, God help it! What may make it fall the wrong way is the influence of the customs of mankind. Custom has more force than reason, though it rarely has sense. It is an attitude of mind and an attitude which is fed by accepting the dogma that the days that are gone were good: and to find strength and warmth, that attitude needs to be constantly brought into association with things that are gone or should be gone. And that, at heart, is one of the primary causes for the preservation of old buildings. It is the desperate clinging to the old, the desperate effort to believe that things have not changed after all.

The last argument will have two effects. Either opponents will hold up their hands in horror and cry 'revolutionary', or they will smile and whisper 'almost a border line case'.

But if I have sown just a few seeds of doubt in their hearts, I shan't mind.

A modern labour-saving house, with plenty of light and air. Such houses are healthy, convenient and comfortable.—J.S.

Or this—again designed for health and usefulness, but without the ultra–modern exterior. Is not this preferable to a worn–out house that has been rejuvenated!—J.S.

Appendix Thirteen

'Urbs in Rure'

by JOHN BETJEMAN

Is West Suffolk to be part of London? This month it is expected that Dr Charles Hill, Minister of Housing and Local Government, will decide.

If he says yes, then four of the most beautiful towns in Britain will be changed out of recognition.

Bury St Edmunds, with its fine flint churches and abbey ruins, its Georgian houses and old theatre and Assembly Rooms, its handsome Corn Exchange and pleasant, narrow shopping streets and wide market place, has only one drawback. It is already overcrowded with traffic. The town is, all the same, a balanced community with all recognized public amenities for a population of just over 20,000. Dr Hill may add 10,000 Londoners to it.

Hadleigh is one of the most perfect small towns in England, with trees, old red brick, flint and plaster and that unassuming beauty of East Anglia which changes to glory in sunlight. It has a population of 3,000, and Dr Hill may double it.

Lavenham and Clare are large villages so famous for the beauty of their churches and old houses that they are in all the guide books to Britain, and much visited by tourists. To each of these villages Dr Hill may add 500 Londoners. The other towns of West Suffolk to be affected are Sudbury, Newmarket, Mildenhall, Brandon, Glemsford, Elmswell, Standon and Haverhill.

West Suffolk was the inspiration of Gainsborough and Constable. Now that Essex has been almost overrun by London, West Suffolk is the nearest unsuburbanized country to the Great Wen. If Dr Hill agrees to its suburbanization 40,000 Londoners will be decanted into it whether they like it or not.

Although this is a tiny fraction of London's population and unlikely materially to solve the problem of London's housing, it will effectively ruin an irreplaceable asset. It will take from us in London the last surrounding deeply pastoral landscape, for in all other directions London and its influence have spread much farther.

The West Suffolk County Council welcomes these 40,000 Londoners. There is the charitable appeal of giving shelter to the homeless. There is much talk of this inundation being inevitable. There is no doubt true sincerity in these remarks for London's housing is indeed a problem. But I suspect that there are other reasons, too. The officials of local authorities naturally see an increase in their influence, possibly a rise in status, as a result of increased rates, and rescue from being absorbed by the larger and more countrified half of the county.

Then the local councillors, who consist, as do most local councils, largely of tradesmen, think that more people will bring more trade. They do not realize that the chain stores and super-markets will put them out of business, and that light industries will drive away local industries.

They maintain that their towns and large villages are stagnant, yet all of those to which it is proposed to add Londoners are increasing in population steadily and naturally. Finally there are probably some farmers, not always the most selfless members of a country community, willing to sell land for housing and industry at a good price.

There is the other side of the picture. The local amenity societies and the Council for the Preservation of Rural England, and many private people who live in West Suffolk have written letters of protest to their local papers. In Lavenham one of the defenders of his home town has sent a letter with 1,447 signatures to the two local MPs.

For once I feel thankful that the fate of West Suffolk, and particularly Bury St Edmunds, Hadleigh, Lavenham and Clare, are not entirely in the hands of the local authorities but Whitehall. The Minister can see that the housing is a national problem. He can realize that country areas of peace and quiet, even if their tender beauty is not so obvious as to be designated a National Park, are essential to the life of the nation.

The noisier and more congested our towns become and the wider our suburbs spread, the more essential are the belts of real country, especially those, like West Suffolk, near a large city. And this is not taking into account the sacrifice of valuable agricultural land or the psychological effect of a large population of bewildered Londoners unused to country life on a settled and natural agricultural community.

Yet the housing of London and our other big cities has to be solved, and Dr Hill's choice is indeed a fearsome one, for we like to live, most of us, in a house of our own with its own bit of garden. Yet if life in England is to be endurable we will have to build more compactly, and quite often higher, in places that are already spreading too far out.

Ugly spreading places could be rebuilt more compactly, with traffic segregated from pedestrian areas. There is less harm in building upwards, if there are pleasure and peace in what is on the ground.

I am also quite certain that putting Londoners into places that are already healthy and happy and balanced communities is taking away something essential and irreplaceable. Once destroyed a glorious wool town of the Middle Ages like Lavenham, and a modest and attractive town like Hadleigh, can never be brought to life. The sad thing is that beauty has become almost an indecent word.

There are many towns and suburbs which can take another 500 people. There is only one Lavenham, only one Clare, only one Hadleigh and only one Bury St Edmunds. Their ruination will not really solve London's housing.

(Reprinted from the *Daily Telegraph*, 19 February 1962)

Select Bibliography

Arnott, W. G., *Alde Estuary*, 1952; reprinted Boydell Press, 1973.
——, *Orwell Estuary*, 1954; reprinted Boydell Press, 1973.
——, *Suffolk Estuary*, 1950; reprinted Boydell Press, 1973.
Barker, Anthony, *The Local Amenity Movement*, The Civic Trust, 1960.
Bury St Edmunds Town Centre Study, Suffolk Preservation Society, 1971.
Cautley, H. Munro, *Suffolk Churches and Their Treasures*, 1938; fourth revised edition, Boydell Press, 1975.
Churches of Suffolk, The, Redundancy and a Policy for Conservation, Suffolk Preservation Society, 1971; reprinted 1972.
Concerning Thorpeness, Suffolk Preservation Society, 1979.
County of Suffolk Surveyed, The, Joseph Hodskinson's map of 1783, with an introduction by D. P. Dymond, Suffolk Records Society, 1972.
Design Guide for Residential Areas, A, Essex County Council, 1973.
Dolman, Peter C. J., *Windmills in Suffolk*, Suffolk Mills Group, 1978.
Dymond, D. P., 'The Suffolk Landscape' in *East Anglian Studies*, ed. L. M. Munby, Heffer, 1968.
Fairbrother, Nan, *New Lives, New Landscapes*, Penguin Books, 1970.
Fincham, Paul, *East Anglia*, Faber & Faber, 1976
——, *The Suffolk We Live In*, George Nobbs, 1976.
Flint, Brian, *Suffolk Windmills*, Boydell Press, 1979.
Glyde, John (ed.), *The New Suffolk Garland*, 1866.
Hoskins, W. G., *The Making of the English Landscape*, Hodder & Stoughton, 1955; Penguin Books, 1970.
——, *One Man's England*, BBC Publications, 1978.
John Constable's Correspondence, vol. I: *The Family at East Bergholt (1897–37)*, Suffolk Records Society, 1962.
Kennet, Wayland, *Preservation*, Temple Smith, 1972.
Maltster, Robert, *Ipswich, Town on the Orwell*, Terence Dalton, 1978.
Newby, Howard, *et al.*, 'Farmers' Attitudes to Conservation', *Countryside Recreation Review*, vol. 2, 1977.
——, *Green and Pleasant Land?*, Penguin Books, 1980.
Oliver, Basil, *Old House and Village Buildings in East Anglia*, Batsford, 1912.
Pevsner, Nikolaus, *Suffolk*, the Buildings of England series, Penguin Books, Revised edition, 1974.
Rackham, Oliver, *Trees and Woodland in the British Landscape*, Dent, 1976.
Redstone, Lilian, *Ipswich through the Ages*, East Anglian Magazine, 1948; reprinted, 1969.
Sandon, Eric, *Suffolk Houses*, Baron Publishers, 1977.
Scarfe, Norman, *The Shell Guide to Suffolk*, Faber & Faber, 1976.
——, *The Suffolk Landscape*, Hodder & Stoughton, 1972.
Steggall, Peter, *East Anglia*, Robert Hale, 1978.
Suffolk Bibliography, A, compiled by A. V. Steward, Suffolk Records Society, 1979.
Suffolk Churches, a Pocket Guide, Suffolk Historic Churches Trust, 1976.
Tennyson, Julian, *Suffolk Scene*, Blackie, 1939; reprinted 1973.
Victoria County History of Suffolk, ed. W. Page, 1911; reprinted 1975.
Young, Arthur, *A General View of the Agriculture of Suffolk*, 1794; reprinted David & Charles, 1969.
Walk Round Lavenham, A, Suffolk Preservation Society, 1977.

Index

(Figures in italic indicate an illustration)